D1552647

Acclaim for *Most Amei*

"In nine skillfully linked essays, Rilla Askew offers Oklahoma history as a microcosm of our national saga as Americans, insisting—and demonstrating—that our personal and state stories fall within national and global narratives. Askew's essays are particularly timely today, her themes playing out in the Black Lives Matter movement and in the violence—and intolerance and hate—seething in the 2016 presidential election campaign. Few books offer such a clear, engaging, and revealing evocation of particular Oklahoma sites and scenes, which Askew repeatedly places within the larger, national, and global frame. *Most American* is an important book, an artful contribution to literature that raises vital issues for Oklahoma and national conversations."

— BARBARA LOUNSBERRY, author of
The Art of Fact: Contemporary Artists of Nonfiction

"In *Most American*, Rilla Askew brilliantly captures her feelings, beliefs, and behaviors about race relations. This book should be read by anyone who is trying to move past clichés and establish positive relationships with individuals who come from cultures different from their own."

— GEORGE HENDERSON, author of
Race and the University: A Memoir

"Rilla Askew—a storyteller of truth and grace in all she writes, whether novel or essay—moves us to compassionately consider Oklahoma in all its faces. Oklahoma's is a rough story of theft and coercion, of beauty and tenderness. In *Most American*, Askew teaches us to see with wiser eyes."

—**JOY HARJO**, author of *Conflict Resolution for Holy Beings: Poems* and *Crazy Brave: A Memoir*

"Rilla Askew shows us the inner workings of a concerned, but generous, critic of our state, Oklahoma. Her style is uniquely gracious even as it rebukes. Though she gives with grit, guilt is never far from the possibility of grace. Every Oklahoman ought to read this book."

—**KEN HADA**, author of *Spare Parts*

MOST AMERICAN

MOST AMERICAN
Notes from a Wounded Place

RILLA ASKEW

Foreword by SUSAN KATES

UNIVERSITY OF OKLAHOMA PRESS : NORMAN

ALSO BY RILLA ASKEW

Strange Business (New York, 1992)
The Mercy Seat: A Novel (New York, 1997)
Fire in Beulah (New York, 2001)
Harpsong (Norman, Okla., 2007)
Kind of Kin (New York, 2013)

Publication details and permission statements for previously published essays
and extracts of other works that appear in this volume are listed on page 162.

LIBRARY OF CONGRESS CATALOGING-IN-PUBLICATION DATA

Name: Askew, Rilla author.
Title: Most American : notes from a wounded place / Rilla Askew.
Description: Norman : University of Oklahoma Press, 2017.
Identifiers: LCCN 2016044853 | ISBN 978-0-8061-5717-7 (pbk. : alk. paper)
Subjects: LCSH: Askew, Rilla. | Askew, Rilla—Homes and haunts—Oklahoma. |
    Authors, American—20th century—Biography. | Oklahoma—Social conditions.
Classification: LCC PS3551.S545 Z46 2017 | DDC 814/.54 [B] —dc23
LC record available at https://lccn.loc.gov/2016044853

The paper in this book meets the guidelines for permanence and durability of
the Committee on Production Guidelines for Book Longevity of the Council on
Library Resources, Inc. ∞

Copyright © 2017 by Rilla Askew. Published by the University of Oklahoma Press,
Norman, Publishing Division of the University. Manufactured in the U.S.A.

All rights reserved. No part of this publication may be reproduced, stored in
a retrieval system, or transmitted, in any form or by any means, electronic,
mechanical, photocopying, recording, or otherwise—except as permitted under
Section 107 or 108 of the United States Copyright Act—without the prior written
permission of the University of Oklahoma Press. To request permission to repro-
duce selections from this book, write to Permissions, University of Oklahoma
Press, 2800 Venture Drive, Norman OK 73069, or email rights.oupress@ou.edu.

1 2 3 4 5 6 7 8 9 10

To the memory of my parents,
Paul and Carmelita Askew.
The best of what's best in us.

*The one who can interpret Oklahoma
can grasp the meaning of America
in the modern world.* —ANGIE DEBO

CONTENTS

FOREWORD

Susan Kates

Any reader of Rilla Askew's fiction knows that it encapsulates American history in microcosm. The colonializing of Indian land, unsavory political skirmishes, and boomtown industrialization took place in the United States over a period of centuries. In Oklahoma, the overnight evolution of this latecomer state is so fresh, we are reminded that its history and culture are an American drama, set on the stage of the fairly recent past.

For Oklahoma and for the United States, there can be no tale that is not rendered in shadow and light. A story of place without attention to its shortcomings as well as its merits is empty boosterism. Many of us have witnessed Askew's unflinching gaze at Oklahoma's flaws and fortunes in her other works. Whether she writes of ethnic cleansing in the 1921 Tulsa Race Riot, crooked oilmen, or afflicted dust-bowler vagrants wandering the country, Askew shows us that Oklahoma's young, chaotic history and its people cannot be known through blind love. She observes her home and its inhabitants like a mother who takes her beautiful, unruly, and guilty child by the shoulders, staring him boldly in the face until the secret is out.

How fitting it is, then, that Askew should now bravely turn that same unflinching eye upon herself. She appears in this book in pivotal moments of her life in Oklahoma and away from it, emerging as a person who knows she is as much a product of place, history, and culture as her fictional characters—Althea in *Fire in Beulah*, Sharon in *Harpsong*, and Mattie in *The Mercy Seat*.

In *Most American: Notes from a Wounded Place*, Askew journeys, in a series of rich and powerful essays, through her childhood and young adulthood to where she stands now. She recognizes, as Ralph Ellison does (via Heraclitus), that geography is fate. Askew writes: "It's hard not to regret the poverty of my upbringing . . . the intellectual, spiritual, experiential poverty that caused me to see the world only through the prism of whiteness." Whether she is interviewing James Brown as a naïve high school journalist or "playing Indian" unconsciously as a young actress in a Trail of Tears outdoor drama, she is unafraid to scrutinize herself in the manner in which she has scrutinized Oklahoma in her fiction.

Askew moved through place and time to acquire the necessary distance to forcefully critique geography and cultural constraints by way of an activist literary tradition. In the poem "Deep Second," Ellison returns to Deep Deuce to listen to "the world-passion behind that old back-alley song / Which sings through my speech more imperious than trumpets or blue train sounds." He longs to speak to a new generation from Deep Deuce to "tell them a story / Of their promise / And their glory." If Ellison had the chance, he "Would sing them a song / All cluttered with my love and regret / And my forgiveness."

Like Ellison and others who longed to leave Oklahoma and start fresh in a new place, Askew found that Oklahoma never left her. Since she was six years old, she has tried to run away from home. In one essay she divulges how she and a neighbor boy walked toward the town dump in Bartlesville, hoping to catch two horses in a nearby pasture and ride them to California; and how at eighteen, she attempted to hitchhike to the Woodstock music festival in New York. But each time, she was apprehended and brought back. As a young woman, Askew did at last leave Oklahoma to become a New Yorker, only to find that her stories lay deeply tethered to the only state with the sound of home in its name: Okla-home-a. The state and its history haunted her, pursued her, until she had no choice but to turn herself west and turn her ear to the ground where the stories were—and listen. By facing Oklahoma's history full on, Askew confronts herself and the profoundly embedded history and culture within her.

Askew is so wholly anchored in the landscapes, weather, and rhythms of Oklahoma that she regards all places she ventures with her birthplace as touchstone. Her intense tie to her roots raises the question, what do people do without some kind of foundation, some inner gauge of place? As they wander the world, how can they travel without a geographical standard to which to hold all other locations? In moments, this collection of essays confirms that Askew was once precisely this kind of person. Or at least she tried to be. Those of us who love her fiction are grateful that she did in fact discover that the stories she most wanted to tell are about Oklahoma. These essays, like all of Askew's writing, prove to be a richly webbed road map we can use to judge where we are in the complex cartography of America. Like the natural and manmade markers of place—the Wichitas, the Tallgrass Prairie Preserve, the Oklahoma National Memorial—Askew's writing reminds us that wherever we go, Oklahoma goes with us.

MOST AMERICAN

Front page of the *Tulsa World*, May 31, 1995. *(Author's collection.)*

Security tag the author was issued in order to work at City Church during recovery operations following the Oklahoma City bombing, April 1995. *(Author's collection.)*

MOST AMERICAN

Who knows but that, on the lower frequencies,
I speak for you?   —RALPH ELLISON, *Invisible Man*

In 1994, Rand McNally accidentally left Oklahoma out of the index to its national road atlas. That same year, as the winter snows outside my house in upstate New York climbed toward one hundred inches and the daytime temperatures sat stubbornly near zero, I began to talk of escaping to Oklahoma. My friends in the frozen Catskills exclaimed, "But isn't it *cold* out there?" They seemed to imagine Oklahoma existing in an area vaguely north of Nebraska and south of the Dakotas. Americans aren't noted for their geographical acuity, but Oklahoma's elusiveness in the public mind goes beyond a lack of knowledge: there has long been an almost mystical anonymity to the place.

Before 1995, Oklahoma kept its invisibility well: we were an indefinable vowel-state located somewhere in the middle of the country, a place recalled, if at all, mainly through the catchy show tune of the same name. Even now, on the Weather Channel, Oklahoma is generally where reporters stand to discuss the fronts moving through the rest of the United States. Calls for submissions from southwestern writers often do not include Oklahoma; nor do calls for writers from the West, or the Midwest, or the South. These regions don't claim us, although Oklahoma borders, and reflects, all of them. It's as if each region shrugs and says to itself, "No, it's no part of us; it must belong to them over there."

Growing up in Oklahoma, I silently agreed. My home state seemed to me then a black hole in the center of the country, a literal and figurative no-man's-land. I came of age biding my time till I could shake its dust off my heels and make for the coast, because I knew very well that the real world was "out there."

My sense of Oklahoma's unimportance, its lack of grandeur or glamour or coolness, was acute but hardly surprising. I'd been molded by a literature created primarily by outsiders, educated to a sanitized, romanticized version of Oklahoma's past, coupled with a half-suppressed history curtailed by the state's own lawmakers, teachers, and civic leaders, and all of this largely unknown to me. What I've come to understand, and what I wish I'd been told as a girl growing up here, is that, far from being a blank spot in the middle of the nation, Oklahoma *is* America: we are its microcosm; our story is America's story, intensified to the hundredth power.

For a time after the 1995 bombing of the Murrah Federal Building, it seemed the rest of the country understood this. The name Oklahoma City, like Ruby Ridge and Waco before it, and Columbine to follow, came to represent far more than a place; it came to stand in the mind of the nation as an elliptical shorthand for the awful event of the bombing itself, for domestic terrorism, the rise of American right-wing militias, and, because of the behavior of Oklahomans in the aftermath, an opportunity for the nation to be proud of itself. For many weeks after the bombing, the Oklahoma character—or that portion of it available to the camera's eye, witnessed on television screens in living rooms and airports and sports bars around the country—was claimed by the whole of the United States.

To be swept from near invisibility to the public stage within seconds by a single act of psychopathic violence is an iconic American story, as the entire drama of the Oklahoma City bombing, from the most horrid detail to the noblest action, is a distinctly American story. As Oklahoma itself is America's story. The media sensed this; they tried to put a face to it, an identity, a name. They called us "America's Heartland," and I think most Americans, and most Oklahomans, believed it. In my view, they got the idea right but the anatomy wrong. This state that had long been a cipher and a mystery, and, like an illegitimate child, was unclaimed by any region, is not the heartland: it is the viscera, the underbelly, the very gut of the nation.

An acquaintance of mine, who originated from Long Island and had traveled widely, found herself living for a time in a small town in southeastern Oklahoma; she told me it was the most foreign country she'd ever been in. And that is true, too. In language and history and culture, Oklahoma is such an extreme distillation of what has taken place on this continent over the past five hundred years that it is nearly unrecognizable to the rest of the nation. Too southern to be midwestern, too western to be southern, too midwestern to be purely southwestern, Oklahoma has kept the secret of its identity as a chameleon does. To the degree we've been seen by outsiders at all, it's been in stereotype: Curly and Laurey, the Joads, tornados and trailer trash, cowboys and Indians, dust—worn one-dimensional sketches that we ourselves have been too willing to adopt. But like Thomas Wolfe's Brooklyn that only the dead can know, Oklahoma is an enigma, a will-o'-the-wisp that can be recognized only slantwise, in relation to its mystery; it is never, I think, what it seems to be.

This is the land that gave birth to twentieth-century America's premier athlete, a Sac and Fox Indian, Jim Thorpe; its definitive white workingman's hero, Woody Guthrie; one of its most celebrated black novelists, Ralph Ellison; and its deadliest pogrom, the Tulsa Race Riot, all within a few dozen years and a hundred miles of one another. Oklahoma is the only place, anywhere, that ever spawned a committed struggle to create an all-black and an all-Indian state, and yet the first laws enacted by our virgin legislature after statehood were Jim Crow. Still, we have more incorporated black towns than any other state in the nation. Still, more Native tribes survive and thrive here than anywhere on the continent, but with the added irony that in Oklahoma they don't live on reservations: in the Land of the Red People, Indians have lost most of their land.

Oklahoma's history is a compressed, ironically inverted miniature of the national narrative, unfolding in a matter of days and weeks and months—sometimes hours—rather than decades, beginning with the Trail of Tears. Our schoolchildren receive a sanitized version of that history, one that is justifiably eloquent about the heroic survival of the Cherokee people but seldom mentions the other tribal nations that suffered equally in being forced to come here, and who have survived just as nobly. The Trail of Tears is never named in our history books for what it was: the United States' largest-scale government-sanctioned bureaucratically administered program of ethnic cleansing. Native people died by the thousands during the Removals, and some of the histories tell us that, but they seldom tell how, within only a few decades after that suffering, this new "Indian Territory" was legislated out of Indian hands. We celebrate again and again the dramatic reenactment of the land runs, but aren't told what those runs meant for tribal people already settled here. We learn about Oklahoma's oil boom, but not about the Osage Reign of Terror, when dozens of Indian people were assassinated for the sake of oil greed.

In terms of numbers and attitude and collective forgetfulness, Oklahoma is predominantly white; it is profoundly religious, politically conservative, inextricably rooted to the land. And this land, a vast skyscape of mountains and lakes and prairies, is peopled with descendants of pioneers and mountain folk, slaves and Indians, entrepreneurs and oil barons, coal miners, immigrants, farmers, cowboys, and outlaws—an inheritance that is like the rest of the country's, except that in Oklahoma, we're hardly a hundred years removed from these roots. Like southerners, we speak a language that is richly accented and idiomatic, and like midwesterners, we still hold the prairie habit of neighbor helping neighbor, even as we carry a ferocious western notion of independence that makes us suspicious of federal control and interference from lawmakers. Some of America's most superb fine artists, from ballerina Maria Tallchief to sculptor Willard Stone, come from this state where children die at the hands of their parents at twice the rate of the rest of the nation. Good-natured friendliness is the dominant trait of a people who were among the first to enact a law allowing private citizens to carry concealed handguns.

Paradox and dichotomy dominate Oklahoma's character, and this is part of what accounts for our mystery, for why we cannot be classified, categorized. Paradox doesn't lend itself readily to sound bites or to easy history lessons. Our story is a study in self-contradiction: unity and division, widespread socialism and reactionary politics, Christian faith and outlaw culture, neighborly helpfulness and murderous greed. If one tries to capture who we are simplistically, with a single cohesive viewpoint, looking only at what is best in us, the effort is doomed to failure. Yet it seems that this is exactly what was handed down to me, a one-dimensional understanding of who we are: a half-truth version of Oklahoma's story. And half the truth, of course, is no truth at all.

I wish I'd been told that ethnic cleansing was the founding condition of my state, about the conflagration that took place in

Tulsa in 1921. I wish someone had told me that Woody Guthrie was a worthy native son, as worthy of honor as our other famous native son, Will Rogers. I would have liked to grow up knowing that Woody was a genuine folk hero—not just Oklahoma's but the nation's. I knew he was from Okemah—I had an aunt and uncle who lived there, and we visited often—but I thought we were supposed to be ashamed that Woody Guthrie came from Oklahoma because he was supposedly a communist, although we sang "This Land Is Your Land" in our school.

I wish I'd been told about Oklahoma's Progressive past, our Socialist past, as well as the facts about the sudden rise and almost as sudden disappearance of the Ku Klux Klan here, or that there were more female Klan members in Oklahoma than in any other state, or that one of our early governors was impeached in part because of his opposition to the Klan. I wish I'd known about the Green Corn Rebellion, that ill-fated, courageous, perhaps foolish rebellion of Native, black, and white Oklahomans who resisted the draft, the jingoism and false patriotism that led the country into the First World War.

Growing up Baptist in this deeply segregated state, I wish someone had told me that the very first Baptist church here was founded by two African Americans, one Native American, and one Anglo American—a blending of the races that is so distinctively Oklahoma's story, as it is fundamentally the American story. Scott Malcomson, in his study of race in America, *One Drop of Blood*, writes of the great experiment of race in Oklahoma; he speaks of what he calls America's three founding races, and returns many times to Oklahoma in order to examine how those forces of race played out here, but as a young person growing up in this state, I had no idea how dramatic, how singular, that story was. I knew nothing about Oklahoma's black towns or the proposed state of Sequoyah or the post-Reconstruction expectation among African Americans that Oklahoma would finally be the Promised Land. It was not until I came to adulthood and read the essays of Ralph Ellison that I learned that the "Territory" toward which Huckleberry Finn lights out at the end of his adventures was *our* Indian Territory—that is, Oklahoma. No educator or parent or preacher told me that.

It's not surprising that we teach only part of our history. To look at one's own transgressions requires great spiritual and emotional maturity, and this is as true for a people or a nation as it is for an individual.

Our natural impulse is to open our eyes only to what's best in us, to own that part and no other. The nation remembers the three thousand victims of the September 11th attacks, a necessary remembrance, but one that says these attacks on civilians were an exception, an unforgivable atrocity, a new kind of warfare, while simultaneously choosing to forget the hundreds of thousands of civilians who died at the hands of America in Dresden and Tokyo, in Hiroshima and Nagasaki. Just so do we in Oklahoma memorialize the 168 innocents who died in the Murrah Building, while carefully, consciously, legislatively choosing not to acknowledge the unnamed, uncounted citizens who died in Tulsa in 1921. To me there is more than a bit of neat numerical bookending in the fact that 2005 marked the tenth anniversary of the Oklahoma City bombing and the fiftieth anniversary of Hiroshima and Nagasaki.

In April 1995, a few days after the bombing, I drove to Oklahoma City. My purpose, like that of thousands of others who came, was to try, in my pain and grief and bafflement, to do something to help, though I had only a dim idea what that might be. When I pulled off I-35 in the late afternoon, I was deeply uneasy, fearful of intruding, disquieted by the surreal aspect of downtown. The streets were nearly empty. There were no rubberneckers, no gawkers, no hustlers or hawkers trying to con a buck from the merely curious, none of the opportunistic hustling my years in New York had taught me to expect. Nor were there as yet the grieving witnesses who would come later, to stand outside the fence and look on in silence, to lay wreaths and notes and teddy bears. On that spring afternoon, at what should have been nearly rush hour, the whole of Oklahoma City seemed abandoned. There was almost no traffic. I saw no pedestrians, no cops. Yes, there were blue sawhorses and yellow strips of police tape lining the perimeter of the bombing site; there were people in uniforms and bright slickers scattered along the approaches to the Murrah Building; but the other streets were empty, and although I expected at any moment to be directed away, to be told, "If you have no official business here, ma'am, you're going to have to leave," in fact, no one told me I had no right to be there. As I drove the quiet streets, located the gutted too-small semi-loaf of the Murrah Building in the distance, parked my car, and walked in that peculiar engineless silence toward City Church, where I'd heard I might be able to help feed rescue workers, I was struck by the incredible restraint of Oklahomans to put aside their curiosity and anger; to come to help, if they might, or to stay away, out of respect and a profound sense of decency, if they could not.

One legacy of the Murrah bombing is that no event since the Second World War, none so rooted in place, so tied to America's idea of itself, so heedless of race and class and our other unnamed divisions, had done for America, in that time, what the actions of the people of Oklahoma City did: allowed us to remember what is right about us. In a terrible way, it made us glad—not glad about the destruction or the unspeakable grief of the victims' families, of course, nor glad to understand for the first time how vulnerable we are—but glad to remember that we can be willing to risk our lives to save the life of another; to believe that at the moment of highest duress, we will behave with honor, we'll forget race, forget fear; that the American character retains the capacity for dignity, willingness, self-sacrifice.

That evening I watched trays of food pour into City Church, sent by individuals, civic groups, businesses, till the church kitchen counters were filled to overflowing and we had to throw much of it away. I saw the too-many willing hands reaching to do the too-little work, people struggling to find a way to contribute, in the same way thousands had stood in line for hours on the day of the bombing waiting to give blood, though there would be tragically too few survivors to receive it. I was moved by these people—my people—even as I couldn't help but be aware of a kind of unspoken hierarchy among the volunteers, defined by who traveled inside the perimeter and who did not. I listened to a young society matron enthuse about having the met the governor at one of her volunteer efforts, saw young men swagger as they drove the empty streets in their humming golf carts, decked officially in Day-Glo slickers, holding walkie-talkies to their lips to report on the coffee needs of the rescue workers. I saw the self-conscious nature of the people's giving, their secret pride in themselves. In an age when no tragedy is too sacred for the camera's eye, even the best must suffer the postmodern curse of Self watching self.

At dawn the next day, seated at a typewriter in a featureless fluorescent-lit room in an undamaged building a few blocks from the bombing site, typing up name tags for workers who would go inside the perimeter, I watched the solemn faces of men and women just coming off the graveyard shift at their jobs—telephone workers, Tinker Air Field workers, postal workers, including a bunch from the U.S. Post Office in Edmond, where a similar, smaller-scale tragedy had played out years before—and I saw, not that unconscious pride, but grief and a deeply unassuming humility. They stood in line patiently, these weary, determined, sorrowing men and women, waiting to be cleared by FBI security, to have their names and tiny Polaroid photos laminated and pinned to their jackets before they turned to walk out into the thin daylight, after having worked a full night's shift, to labor the whole day among the mangled remains. They came to work tirelessly, in a hopeless endeavor, because the thing had been so terrible, so horrifically wrong, and they had to work to fix it right. In this way, as in the other, they proved to be quintessentially American.

Oklahomans reflect the whole of the American paradox: our selflessness and keen self-absorption, our conservatism and revolutionary impulses, our modernity and deep ingrainedness in the past. We are a generous people, compassionate, hardworking, self-sacrificing, capable of great heroism, decent. Violent. Filled with prejudice. Profoundly and pridefully independent. Sentimental.

In the days immediately following the September 11th attacks, I walked my Catskills country road under jeweled autumn skies with a familiar pain and fear and bafflement in my chest, a déjà vu–like sense of already having lived through this. In Lower Manhattan the rescue efforts continued, the victims' families waited and hoped and prayed, but I knew there would be no more survivors pulled from the rubble. I knew how quickly the unthinkable would become the new reality, how the nation's mind would open to accept the unacceptable, and close around it. That the pain and grief would soon turn to a cry for vengeance for many, and, for the few, to the principle of forgiveness, a seeking for peace. I knew that the site of the destruction would become both sacred ground and a source of division and controversy. This sense of familiarity is one I believe many Oklahomans shared. It seemed to me then, seems to me now, that 9/11 was one more way in which our story is the nation's story.

As a writer I can't help but see connections between events, the narrative through-line that runs beneath coincidence, the rhythmic resonance of numerical divisions. In that sense, it seems to me now unsurprising that Oklahoma would have been the site of the horrific 1995 explosion that was the prelude to our current age of terrorism, but with the added twist that in Oklahoma City, it wasn't foreign terrorists who killed Americans, but the nation's own turning against her own.

The bomb that destroyed the Murrah Building was composed of fertilizer and diesel fuel, two substances woven into Oklahoma's story, reflecting the farming and oil industries that have shaped us. The men who conceived each of those terrorist assaults—the Oklahoma City bombing and the 9/11 attacks—had become radicalized by the same event, in the same time period: the 1991 Gulf War. Osama bin Laden developed his supreme hatred for the United States because of American military stationed in Saudi Arabia in the time of the Gulf War: the very war in which Timothy McVeigh learned the unleashing of violence, learned terms like "collateral damage," which he used to describe the children who died in the Murrah bombing. And that first Gulf War, although it had other named justifications, was finally a war about the struggle to control oil, a world-sized reflection of one portion of Oklahoma's story we'd like not to remember: the shameful, terrorizing, often murderous theft of oil rights from our own Freedmen and Native people.

The blueprint McVeigh used for the bombing was a white-supremacist polemic, *The Turner Diaries*, which outlined a terrorist act very like the Murrah bombing—and what was the goal of that fictional terrorist action, and, implicitly, McVeigh's goal? An American race war. And in fact the nearest thing to an American race war did take place in Oklahoma, in Tulsa, in 1921. That event has been called different names—the Tulsa Race Riot, the Burning, the Tulsa Disaster—but it bears many of the worst characteristics of ethnic war: armed conflict, wild rumor, the imputation to the other side of one's own worst acts, the profound silence and collective forgetfulness that follows. Still, one of the most enduring images of the Oklahoma City bombing, preserved in photographs of the victims and survivors, the children and adults, grieving family members, rescue workers, is how completely and harmoniously racially mixed the people are. And so the circles go, the twists and inversions, the connections and parallels.

And yet when I look at the story, I see at the heart of it perhaps the greatest paradox of all: after the bombing, Oklahoma became idealized as what's best in America—the "Oklahoma standard," it was called— and yet in many ways we continue to be anonymous in the mind of the nation. Seen and not seen. Mythologized and virtually invisible. April 19, 1995, is understood as a watershed date, like December 7, 1941, and November 22, 1963, and September 11, 2001: a cataclysmic turning point at which America lost her innocence. Except of course we were never innocent, merely cocooned from half our history. The truths of theft, slavery, genocide, the nation's founding core of violence remain in our soil and blood and memory, whether we choose to look at them or not.

But why look at these old buried sorrows? What does it matter that we teach our children only part of our story? We don't, as a state or a nation, do such things anymore. Or so we want to tell ourselves. Part of the American paradox is that, on the one hand, we delight in stories of redemption, tales that reflect "the triumph of the human spirit," that remind us of the old verities William Faulkner spoke about in his Nobel Prize acceptance speech: love and honor and pity and pride and compassion and sacrifice. On the other hand, we subscribe to a pitiless, senseless western myth of redemption through violence. Both impulses are simplistic, romantic, sentimental. Sentiment, in its subtlety, can be a grave enemy. It looks at one side only, hides its face from unpleasantness, from responsibility. To surrender to it is to forget that redemption is earned. It cannot be won without repentance, and repentance, in the old Hebrew understanding, means to turn away from *with knowledge*. One cannot repent what one will not own. This is as true spiritually for a nation or a people as it is for the individual soul.

I hunger for the old verities as Faulkner outlined them; I believe them to be the dominant traits that characterize us, as Americans, as Oklahomans. But I believe, too, that there is a spiritual law that says we cannot be forgiven until we are willing to forgive, and that we will not find in our hearts forgiveness for those who have wronged us until we have owned our own part.

Oklahoma's pain of April 19, 1995, presaged the nation's pain on September 11, 2001, in the same way our past encapsulates, exagger- ates, intensifies America's past. Just so, I believe Oklahoma's spiritual future could predict America's future. If we as a people were to turn from sentiment to the task of owning our whole history; if we were to begin to make amends for past wrongs, first of all by owning them, and then by turning away from them with knowledge; if we were to teach our children the whole truth of who we are and who we have been, Oklahoma could become the conscience of the nation. It would hardly matter then whether the rest of the country recognized us. In fact, it's not good to become too conscious of one's conscience, is it? The still, small voice, we call it. And we are, after all, the nation's underbelly, the source of the lower frequencies Ralph Ellison wrote about.

The author with Joe Dale Tate Nevaquaya, Catskills, spring 1993. *(Author's collection.)*
Joe Dale in the hammock, Catskills, spring 1993. *(Author's collection.)*

BLOODMEMORY

*There is a field / of talking blood / that I have
not been able / to reach, / not even with knives, /
not yet.*   —JOY HARJO, "Alive"

In my novel *The Mercy Seat*, a white family leaves their Kentucky
home abruptly in 1887, traveling west in a covered wagon with all their
belongings and dogs and children, knowing—at least some of them—
that they will never return home again. The seeds of the tale came to
me through my own family's story, told to me by my elders: how my
great-great-grandfather and his brother fled Kentucky in the middle
of the night because they had broken the laws there. They took their
families and headed west to Indian Territory, where, as non-Indian
people, they had no legal right to own land. The book begins:

> There are voices in the earth here, telling truth in old stories. Go
> down in the hidden places by the waters, listen: you will hear
> them, buried in the sand and clay. Walk west in the tallgrass
> prairie; you'll hear whispering in the bluestem. Stand here, on
> the ragged rim of a mountain in the southeastern corner; you
> can hear the sound rising on the south wind, sifting in the dust
> through the crowns of the cedars: stories told in old voices, in the
> pulse of bloodmemory; sung in the hot earth above the ceaseless
> thrum of locusts and nightbirds whillowing, beneath the faint
> rattle of gourd shells. One story they tell is about longing, for this
> is a place of homesickness. The land has become home now, and
> so the very core of this land is sorrow. You can hear it longing
> for the old dream of itself. Like this continent. This country.
> *Oklahoma.* The very sound of it is home.

Bloodmemory. I first heard that term from my friend, the poet and artist Joe Dale Tate Nevaquaya. It was dusk. We were sitting beneath a faintly glowing summer sky in his mother's backyard in Oklahoma City. Joe held out his arm, turned his wrist skyward. This is where it is remembered, he said.

Joe Dale had been raised by his Yuchi grandmother in the tiny Creek County community of Gypsy. His grandmother was one of the last of the pureblood Yuchis, one of the last fluent speakers of the Yuchi language. She didn't speak any English but communicated with her grandsons entirely in their native tongue. Until Joe started school in Bristow at the age of six, he was able not only to under-stand his language but to speak it. But that evening, long years later, when we sat in the yard talking, his mother tongue was lost to him. Like spider webs clotting his throat, he told me. Clogging his mind. Almost remembered, he said, making a gesture near his head. Here, though, he said, turning his wrist, I remember. And he went on to talk about bloodmemory, what is known in the blood, in the spirit, beyond knowing. He was speaking of his native language, stolen from him, yes, but also the collective memory of all that had passed among his people from the time they lived in their homeland in what is now Georgia, through the tragedy of the Removals, when the Yuchis were marched west on the Trail of Tears and enrolled with the Mvskoke (Creek) people, all the way to that summer night in 1991, in a backyard in Oklahoma City. I felt then, as Joe talked, a kind of piercing mystery, an unfathomable knowledge beyond words, beyond translation, outside conceptualization. We know so much more than we understand that we know. This is what Joy Harjo's poems say to me, insistent as the rhythmic pulse of a heartbeat, every time I read them.

"Nothing can be forgotten," she writes in her prose poem "Autobi-ography," "only left behind. . . . Dreams aren't glass and steel but made from the hearts of deer, the blazing eye of a circling panther. Trans-lating them was to understand the death count from Alabama, the destruction of grandchildren, famine of stories. . . . It's in our blood."

Researchers tell us that violence inflicted on one's forebears is car-ried to later generations, embedded in genetic code, handed down, like eye color, from generation to generation. They call it by many names.

Transgenerational trauma. Intergenerational transmission of violence. Historical wounding. These researchers are only now describing what Indian people have been saying for, well, all time: that memories are not just borne in the mind, nor alone in the spirit (though, yes, they are borne there, too), but in the blood and bones. Racial trauma may be transmitted epigenetically, the researchers say. Here, my Yuchi friend says, turning his veins skyward, is where it is remembered. And what of the violence our forebears inflicted on others? Is this carried, too, within our genetic code? The question haunts me. It informs, on some level, every word I write.

When I think of Joe Dale talking that night, I have a forceful sense that for Native people, it is not only trauma preserved and handed down through generations but an entire way of being, a genetic and soul-borne reality that endures despite centuries of violence and warfare and calculated, cruel, mind-numbing bureaucracy aimed at eradicating every bit of Indianness from the people themselves. "Kill the Indian and save the man," the U.S. army officer who founded Carlisle Indian School famously said. They haven't done so yet. The resistance and endurance of this land's indigenous peoples have remained beyond all efforts to eradicate them. Still, some tribes have been entirely annihilated. Still, there are layers of loss beyond words, beyond measure. Nearly beyond bearing.

In the spring of 1993, Joe Dale came to visit me in upstate New York. I was teaching at Syracuse University then, a visiting professor, and I had invited him to give a public reading of his stunningly powerful poetry and also visit my class in Native American literature. He stayed a few weeks. We walked the too-cold-for-spring streets; took a road trip to Buffalo, where Joe gave another reading at an art gallery; sat for hours smoking cigarettes and laughing in the front room of the little house I rented in Syracuse. We drove north to visit the home of our friend Sandy Cook on the Akwesasne Mohawk Nation Reserve, which straddles the U.S.–Canadian border. It was after that trip to Akwesasne, I believe, that Joe and I sat one evening in a coffee shop in Syracuse, near campus, talking about loss. That loss. That unspeakable loss. Unrecoverable. Untranslatable. Joe spoke again about the loss of his language, the spider webs clotting his throat, and for an instant I felt it, in the same way I'd grasped, if only for a fleeting instant, the sense of bloodmemory when he said it that evening in his mother's yard. A while later I wrote Joe this poem:

MOTHER TONGUE

You were six, then, when they stole your tongue.
My mind had seen a vacuum theft, your throat
stripped dry of words, a searing, powdered,
sucking death, a bone-dry theft, your language
plucked from jaw and tongue.

It never was this way.

We sat inside a coffee cave in Syracuse,
that north gray place, and as you spoke
in frictive tongue (the one they gave
for Yuchi words), and told again this loss
and rage, my body welled, a backwash swell,

a tide of black and water. A fullness then, a dark
wet sense, the tissues soft with waiting. I knew
this sense, or something like: the tense wet weight
before the blood, or pregnant once, with blighted
egg that never would breathe form.

I knew this sense, or something like, in woman's
ways, the way I could: the swollen dark,
the tick-gorged swell of loss and expectation.
In coffee dark, that womblike place, my body
dreamed another way. They did not suck

Your words from you but turned it 'round, reversed:
They stuffed their wadding down your throat, their
viscous words of tooth and tongue, and tamped them
down, to stuff you full, their language crammed and
clotted, to crowd your words in dark wet void:

Not vacuumed, gone, not dry or dead, but living dark,
  And waiting.

So much is known beyond knowing. So much is lost. There is yet a world hidden from us, blacked out, expunged—from the histories, from our collective memories, even from bloodmemory, I believe. It is in the lost places that I've sought my voice as a writer. "This is a place of homesickness," the story begins, ". . . and so the very core of this land is sorrow."

Oklahoma's tale has always been one of loss and expectation, just as it has been a narrative of migration and restless movement. Before European invaders began to pass through this territory in search of golden cities and fur-trading routes, the Caddo and Wichita peoples were settled here, but even they left their villages in summer to follow the great bison herds. It was not long before these passages of Spaniards and Frenchmen led, inexorably, to the destruction of the Caddoan civilizations, and then, for a time before the Removals, these lands were hunting grounds for the Osage and Quapaw in the east, the Kiowa and Comanche in the west. But the forced migration and reset-tlement of the Five Tribes brought a new wave of inhabitants, followed quickly by the invasion of white settlers pounding south in the land runs, the droves of black Exodusters migrating here toward promise. The elemental hope and loss of leaving one's homeland—emigration—and entering a new land—immigration—are the very substance of the American story. They're the substance of Oklahoma's story. From the Trail of Tears to *The Grapes of Wrath*, our most iconic narratives have been about how this land, this Oklahoma, is a place so many have come to in pain and anticipation and sorrow, and it is a place others have left in just the same way. I believe these tales of migration and immigration, of longing and hope, of loss and expectation, are embed-ded in me—they are in my DNA.

I've been longing for home all my life. Even as a small child playing in the rustling fields behind our house at the edge of the tallgrass prairie west of Bartlesville, every time the wind would whip up—that balmy south wind blowing up from the Gulf, portending change—my heart would be filled with a terrible yearning: the ache of nostalgia for something that had been lost to me in a time, surely, before my five or six years on this earth. So I thought then, and sometimes think now. I tried to grasp what I yearned for, what element whispered in my blood. I understood it to be loss, yes, but of what? The only word that came close to saying it was "home."

And yet, the first time I ran away from home, I was six. A neighbor boy and I walked a half mile to the town dump with the aim of catching two horses pastured in a field there and riding them to California. Fortunately, his young cousin snitched on us, and his aunt came in her car and brought us home. I tried again at eighteen. This time my aim was to meet up with some hippie acquaintances hitchhiking from the West Coast to the Woodstock Festival in upstate New York. But my parents found out that I was staying at a friend's house across town while I waited for these traveling companions to come through. My dad came and got me, and I went home. Later I tried to move to California, several different sojourns that could have been permanent but turned out not to be. It wasn't until 1980 that I finally made my escape: a little before Thanksgiving, I quit my job in Tulsa, sold my pickup, cobbled together a few hundred dollars and a handful of phone numbers, and struck out for Manhattan to become a famous actress. The first thing I did while I was preparing to leave was track down a sublet for a one-room apartment in Hell's Kitchen. The second thing I did was take the money from my last paycheck out to Tulsa International Airport and buy myself a plane ticket home for Christmas. Because I knew, even then, Oklahoma was not going to let me go.

Maybe this paradox is in all of us, this simultaneous compulsion to run away married to an insistent, irreconcilable yearning to return home. For me, it's taken a long time to understand where home is. It's not the oil company town of Bartlesville in northeastern Oklahoma where I grew up, or the Sans Bois Mountains in southeastern Oklahoma where my family has lived for five generations, or the Cherokee Hills around Tahlequah where I lived for years in a cabin on the Illinois River, or Tulsa, where I came into my own as a young adult before I lit out for New York. It's not—though often it feels this way—the vast sky country of the shortgrass prairie that makes my heart lift as soon as, driving west, I see the trees begin to disappear, the horizon open, the sky arch wide and deep above me. "Home" for me is all these places. "*Oklahoma*. The very sound of it is home."

I can't tell you why the pull of this place is so strong; I can only tell you that it is. I'm not the only one who feels it. Plenty of folks in the Okie diaspora will tell you about this longing for home—the wind, the dust, the light, the air. "Great spaces and windy light," as W. B. Yeats described a mythic Ireland. It's how I think of my homeland.

Oklahoma is my center of gravity. It's the source of my work. It's not really what I'm writing *about*, it's the place I write *from*, even in all the years I didn't live here. It's where the voices reside—my spiritual and emotional and geographical center.

Many, many times I've heard Joy Harjo's line from her poem "The Last Song" quoted by other Oklahoma writers: "oklahoma will be the last song / i'll ever sing." In nine words she captures a truth that cuts at the heart of all of us. And yet the frame of that truth is hers alone. I've never heard anyone say those words without giving Joy attribution. Such is her stature among us. Such is the power she has to tell our story—and here I don't mean the story of Oklahoma's writers or citizens or tribal people, I mean America's story. Without her voice, and the voices of all the indigenous writers here, that story is not, in fact, told.

In her essay "The Story of America: A Tribalography," Choctaw novelist/essayist/poet/playwright/scholar LeAnne Howe writes: "Native stories are power. They create people. They author tribes. America is a tribal creation story, a tribalography." Nowhere has the power of Native stories to create the American story been more forceful, more impactful, than this hatchet-shaped space in the belly of the nation, this forty-sixth of the United States, named for two Choctaw words: *okla* (people) *humma* (red). Yet, in the mind of the dominant culture, Native presence here arcs from invisibility to appropriation, and back again.

When I set out to write a novel about the Tulsa Race Riot of 1921, I found that I had to learn my own history first. I had to explore my own ancestral biography, vague and uncertain as it was, to seek out the truth beneath old family stories my people had glossed over or felt uncomfortable to tell—or wouldn't tell at all—in order to understand how racial attitudes were carried into Indian Territory with such force that they created the conditions that led to the worst race war in American history.

My family are southerners. They came, some of them, from Kentucky and Arkansas, but most came from Mississippi. Three sides, both matrilineal and patrilineal, migrated into Indian Territory in the late 1800s from the areas around Sardis and Tupelo, from Faulkner's Mississippi, the old slaveholding South, the original homelands of the Chickasaw people. They traveled west in covered wagons, settled in the valleys of the Sans Bois in the Choctaw Nation. What did they bring with them, borne in the blood and the bone, carried in their habits of being to be handed down to later generations? Tenacity, for one thing. A stunning capacity for hard work. Endurance. Faith—not just religious faith, though that is surely part of the story, but faith in the future, no matter how dark the present might seem. Faith that the land will sustain you, no matter how stony and unyielding the ground. Faith in survival, regardless of what devastating forces nature may throw at you: drought, fire, flood, wind. Resiliency, yes. Yearning—oh, yes. My people carried within them, and handed down to me, this homesickness. This ineffable, unanswerable longing for home. Even when *home* is a place that breaks your heart.

I'm the daughter and granddaughter of Southern Baptist deacons. I grew up on the King James Bible. I grew up listening to stories. My family's roots go deep in this place where stories from the Christian Bible and Native American spiritual worldview collide, blend, permeate all. I write about that abutment, that blending, and tension, how the juxtaposition of their elements must be set in relief, because they are not separate but simultaneous. This is what I understand from our tribalography here. The delving into the past I did, both direct and indirect, taught me how religious faith may shape both the best and the worst in us. How the pioneer grit of my forebears, ground down by poverty and grief, may turn those same pioneers mean as a snake. How the spirit is powerful, ever present, superimposed both over and underneath the visible world. How brother may rise up against brother, in racial hatred or fratricide.

I had to write that story before I could write about the 1921 riot. I needed to understand where the forces of violence come from within us, because, most assuredly, my people carried violence into I.T. as well. This tale of flesh and the spirit became my first novel, *The Mercy Seat*. It is a story of violence and blood sacrifice and the power of the Unseen, like the stories in the King James Bible I grew up with. The biblical mercy seat (in Hebrew *Kapporet*, the "atonement piece") is the gold, cherubim-adorned covering for the Ark of the Covenant, where

Yahweh ordered that the sin offering, sprinkled blood from the blood sacrifice, be laid. *The Mercy Seat* has been called an Old Testament–style book, in part because of that title, which comes from Leviticus, and in part because it tells the story of brother slaying brother, like Cain and Abel in Genesis. It can be read as the story of sinners expelled from the Garden of Eden, continually trying to find their way home. But it is also a novel about how the lives of African Americans, Native Americans, and European Americans intersected in Indian Territory in the late 1800s, and it is a book whose spiritual underpinnings include Choctaw Indian religious worldview. Only after I'd begun to write did I see how forcefully the biblical stories I'd been raised with at once reflected and contradicted stories of the spirit I knew from Indian friends. How the loss of ritual, of ceremony, of pathways and guidance, can cause a soul to be lost. How the understanding I'd always sensed intuitively, inarticulately, beyond the frame of language, is true: there are layers in the spiritual realm that cannot be grasped with the finite mind.

The beginning of the novel finds me wrestling with racial dominance, exploring it through the mind and behavior of a white child, the girl Mattie, no older than ten, who fears, as if by instinct, the Other, and who wields against a black wet nurse, without comprehension or historical knowledge, the power of her white skin—because the story of that dominance, and the tragic lie that to this day supports and gives life to it, is part of what my people carried into Oklahoma, too.

I wrote *The Mercy Seat* between 1993 and 1996, years when I was questing very hard spiritually and at the same time suffering a terrible, nearly incapacitating homesickness that caused me to run back to Oklahoma every chance I could. I had felt that longing during my years in Manhattan, and later Brooklyn, but it was only after my husband and I left the city altogether and moved full time to our cabin in the Catskill Mountains that my longing for Oklahoma grew so acute. I had read how the Apache people, when they were forced from their homelands in the vast southwestern deserts to the dark, densely wooded lowlands of Alabama, said they had to climb trees to see the sun. I imagined them climbing the tallest pines, clambering as high as possible, clinging to the treetops for hours, days, maybe, just so they could *see*—the sky, the horizon. Just so they could breathe. This is how

I felt then, after we moved to the mountains, as if I could not stand up straight, couldn't *see*, couldn't breathe.

And so the novel was born of isolated winter months in our frozen cabin in the Catskills, and from the high, dank heat of August when I spent time in Oklahoma with my family, with Indian friends, listening to their stories, going deep in my own memory, to places I'd forgotten. I remembered the Choctaw woman in Red Oak who took care of my sister and me when we were very little. Her name was Lula Henry, and some of the images the fevered, lost girl Mattie remembers of Thula's face in the novel come from my memories of Lula Henry. I heard my Papaw Allie's voice talking in my head, remembered old stories handed down from both sides of my family: my dad's grandfather sentenced in Judge Isaac Parker's court for smuggling whiskey into Indian Territory, serving time in the same Fort Smith jail as Belle Starr. And on the other side, how my mother's grandfather, the one who was purportedly, or maybe only just maybe, part Choctaw Indian, rode off from home on a horse one day, never to return. I thought, too, sometimes, that I could almost hear a kind of distant, half-perceived music, lingering just there, at the edge of sound. I wrote things I didn't understand. I gave these mysteries to the girl Mattie in the novel, a child gifted in ways that aren't definable in western terms: born to be a shaman, a seer, a conduit to the spiritual world—or so she would have been if she'd grown up in a different circumstance; if she'd had any ritual or teacher to show her how to use the gifts she'd been given, she'd have been a high priestess, a medicine woman, maybe a Joan of Arc. But she has had no guidance. She has only a dead mother and an absent father, self-will, a misunderstood gift, and an overriding obsession to take her mama home.

Sometimes I don't know why I write what I write, and that was true with *The Mercy Seat* more than any of my other novels. I wrote it in a state of surrender, not judging or planning, as I did with later works, but just listening to a kind of inner rhythm, the narrative voices telling the story. That's why the book opens as it does: "There are voices in the earth here, telling truth in old stories." I wrote those lines after the book was finished.

It was also after *The Mercy Seat* was finished, in 1996, that my husband and I bought a home on a ridge in the Sans Bois Mountains in southeastern Oklahoma and began to spend part of each year here, near McAlester, not far from my family's home in Red Oak. I couldn't return to Oklahoma entirely then, but the journey home had begun. All my life I've sought to understand the mystery of patterns, synchronicity, orchestration. The pattern for me has been one of circles and spirals, and a kind of vertical, nonlinear knowledge. We all know so much more than we know that we know. Maybe part of it is bloodmemory, what's borne in the blood, inside our very cells. Or maybe it's just the power of stories handed down from our forebears, half-remembered, half-forgotten, the truth of the past and the present, the voices we seek in the lost places. Or that, in any case, is a place to begin.

The author with (*left to right*) Joe Dale Tate Nevaquaya, Joy Harjo, Richard Ray Whitman, and Jeanetta Calhoun Mish at MELUS poetry reading, Skirvin Hotel, Oklahoma City, March 7, 2014. (*Author's collection.*)

PASSING

The Writer's Skin and the Authentic Self

In the early days of my writing career, which happened to coincide relatively closely with the early days of the World Wide Web, I would from time to time do a little "ego surfing," as my writer friends called it. I'd type my name into the search engine and surf the web to see what folks were saying about me. If I happened to click on, oh, result 72, say—way down past the sites featuring remaindered copies of my books for as little as one penny plus shipping and handling, but a bit before the cemetery lists including dead people bearing my first or last name—I would find "Rilla Askew" on a variety of fiction diversity lists: North American Native authors, American Indian authors. In some places after my name, in parentheses, it would say (Cherokee?). In others, quite declaratively: (Choctaw). Elsewhere I'd be listed as a contemporary African American author. The first two are, so far as I'd always been told, true. The latter is, presumably, not. Although who's to say? America has always been a mestizo nation. A miscegenation nation. The mixing of blood has always been a fundamental truth of our story, although it's not one we've often told ourselves—at least not much before now.

But the fact is, I grew up white in America, with all the privileges and presumptions of whiteness. My slow awakening to what that means has, more than any other single factor, forged my subject as a novelist; it has shaped all that I understand about myself as an American writer. Still, when it comes to being included on diversity lists, I haven't tried to correct or clarify my heritage. Let me do my work, I've thought. Let others believe what they will. But my silence tells a story.

Most often when we speak of "passing," we're talking about race—about crossing the color line for political, social, economic reasons. Generally, we're talking about someone passing for at least some portion of what that person truly is, a literal part of one's heritage. It's true that people do sometimes pass for what they've never been—a different economic class, a different sexual orientation—but usually our physicality determines what we're able to pass for, which means that most often we're passing for a portion of an authentic self, and most often we're passing toward cultural dominance. When it comes to racial passing along a black-white continuum, this has been especially true. In person our bodies go before us. We're wrapped in the integument of America's race history, whether we're aware of it or not. Whether we care about it or not. In person we're defined by our skin color, the shape of our eyes, the texture of our hair. Assumptions are made.

One evening in 2008, I had dinner at the home of a friend in Chicago. He had invited several guests, and they were really all very nice. Nice white people. One of the women made a remark about American Indians, repeating something she had heard from a white friend in Arizona. She wasn't giving her own observations, merely telling us something she'd heard, offering it, in this small gathering of white people, as a perceived truth. "Solipsistic" is one of the words she used. Another woman at the table made an observation about African American young people she'd once worked with in Detroit, saying essentially—although this is not what she thought she was saying—that they need to act white, speak white, dress white if they want to "get ahead" in America. And because my skin is white, these women made assumptions about how I would hear what they were saying. Always, in such situations, there is a shadow me listening, a shadow me whispering, *If I remain silent here, I'm passing—I'm letting them think that I'm like them.* "Hey, you know what?" I said, as if the thought had just occurred to me. "The conditions you're talking about? It's the same with the poor white folks I come from, too."

On that same Chicago visit—I was there for the huge annual gathering of American writers called the Association of Writers and Writing Programs Conference—I met author Michelle Duster. She is a descendant of black activist Ida B. Wells, and her book *Ida Wells in Her Own Words* features some of her famous aunt's writings on class legislation and lynchings, subjects I'm deeply interested in. I wanted to talk with her about that terrible part of American history, but, because of assumptions I made, I found myself working too hard to explain who I am. I'd back up, start over, say the same things in different words, trying to make clear where my heart is. I mentioned my black godchildren like the most blatant of name droppers, all because of suppositions I made about assumptions I assumed that she made, because my skin is white. In the end we had a good talk, but it took an awkward dance on my part before we got there.

But it's among Indian people that I feel most conflicted. When I go to powwows, I don't dance. I stand back as an observer, an outsider, no matter how powerfully the drumming and the singing work on me. When I'm hanging with Indian writer friends, though, I feel a part of, not apart from, and I say "ennit," laugh as they laugh. Mostly, though, among Indian people, I remain silent. When whites ask me if I'm part Indian, they always mention my cheekbones—a peculiarly white construct. The Indians I know don't talk about cheekbones. If they think of me as Indian, it's not because of how I look.

Well, that's the in-person presentation. What about the writer's skin? The notion of writing across race or gender makes for lively forums in the literary world, lots of passionate opinion and controversy. When I write in the voice of an eighty-one-year-old dead white man narrating his own funeral, no one's bothered, and I'm not scared, although I've surely never been an eighty-one-year-old white man, dead or alive. But when I write in the voice of a Creek Freedwoman speaking directly to the reader in the early 1900s, or a Cherokee mother whose son has been killed in a car crash, or when

I'm using a close third-person point of view to create the internal monologue of a young black woman who has just been raped by a white man, I go there in fear and trembling. Because race is America's perpetual hidden wound, as Wendell Berry has said, and it can tear open at the slightest pressure.

Still, I'm always writing about race, because I'm always writing about place. The convergence of America's three founding races in my home territory has dominated our origination story. These are the voices I write in, and quite naturally readers want to know, Is the author black? Is she Indian? Even when readers check my photo on the back of a book, the questions linger.

In Oklahoma, my nebulous heritage is such a common story that is has become a cliché: the mysterious "Cherokee" great-great-grandmother on my dad's side; my mother's supposedly part-Choctaw mother, who called herself Black Dutch to explain her dark hair and eyes and skin. These purportedly Indian forebears are descended from anonymous women—females who passed into the white world so effectively, the story goes, that their bloodlines cannot be traced. But here's the thing: my sisters grew up with these same stories, and they don't think of themselves as part Indian. But I do. Or, at least, let me say this: I did. It's a peculiar phenomenon that streaks through my family—some of us have always thought or felt or believed ourselves to be part Indian, and some have not. When I was a girl growing up with my grandfather's stories, I never doubted. I lived inside the dominant culture, reaping all its benefits, but in my heart I carried that secret claim. My white friends in those days weren't claiming to be Indian. I thought my grandfather was bold to declare we had Indian blood.

Later, when I lived in the Cherokee country around Tahlequah in young adulthood, I felt a strong kinship. Cherokees weren't exotic feather-and-buckskin-wearing fantasies with names like Morning Star and Tonto, they were the Real People Themselves, with names like Betty Smith and John Ross. The fact that my family had no documentation showing Indian blood didn't bother me. We had our stories. If anyone asked if I was part Indian, I'd answer with,

"Well, my Papaw Allie always said . . ." For me, in those days, that was enough. As an individual, I probably could have lived with this amorphous, unverified identity indefinitely, but as a writer, I had to make a choice.

My first published story was a Cherokee story, "The Gift," in *Nimrod*'s "Oklahoma Indian Markings" issue in 1989. It was later collected in *Aniyunwiya/Real Human Beings: An Anthology of Contemporary Cherokee Prose*. I spoke with the anthology's editor, Joe Bruchac, a mixed-blood Abenaki, who'd selected the story. I wound out a long explanation about my Indian heritage being unproven, saying that I don't have a Certificate of Degree of Indian Blood card, but Joe said that in making their determination about who's Indian and who's not, they weren't looking at blood quantum but at whether the writer's primary identification is with the tribe. I didn't know where my primary identification lay—I didn't feel any more a part of the poor white tenant farmers I come from than the Cherokee people I'd lived with around Tahlequah or my Indian artist friends. But I knew that I grew up white. And I knew that I did not want to be a wannabe.

Like the character in Tim O'Brien's *The Things They Carried* who ends up going to the war because he's too much of a coward to be thought a coward, I chose not to claim to be an Indian writer because I did not want to be like other white girls with their Cherokee princess great-grandmothers who so very much wannabe Indian. Anyway, how was I going to claim to be an Indian writer when my fair, freckled sisters don't "feel" Indian? After "The Gift," I never again sought publication in collections of Indian writings. The publishing world likes to categorize; it wants an angle, a genre, a niche. Even if I didn't put "Cherokee" or "Choctaw" after my name, to join with Indian writers would be a silent declaration—a type of passing. My friend Tim Tingle, a wonderful Choctaw writer and storyteller, has said to me, "Let us claim you!" And a Mohawk friend, Sandy Cook, who traveled with me from upstate New York to Oklahoma at a time when I was really struggling with this stuff, said, "Ah, come on, Rilla, you know you're an Indian woman."

Actually, no, I don't. I do, and I don't. Both conditions are simultaneously true, a paradox that is like the essential paradox of America, this racial melting pot where race is our greatest divider. Regardless of which complicated or uncomplicated heritage I claim, I'm still passing. When I go among my white relatives, I'm passing there, too: I drop the *g* from the ends of words, talk about snakes and ticks and the weather. I'm as much an observer and outsider at a family reunion in Red Oak as I am at an African Methodist Episcopal church in Ponca City or a stomp dance in Okfuskee County or a Jamaican birthday party for one of my godchildren in Brooklyn. But I feel at home in all these places, too: a profound sense of belonging.

As a writer, I've never had to pass toward cultural dominance to find acceptance. In America that cultural dominance is changing anyway—a fact that's got a lot of white people worried. But as a novelist, I do have to write from an authentic self, no matter what kind of writer's skin I wear. That writer's skin is, in fact, my own skin, constructed not of traceable blood quantum and genealogical declarations, but of layers of experience and choice—the homeland that has claimed me, the people I've chosen to love. This is where the stories come from.

Still, there are voices in my head, haunting me the way Virginia Woolf said her Angel in the House whispered that she ought not write what her mind and spirit told her to write because she was a woman. In my case it's the voice of an Indian writer crying out at a reading, "Let us tell our own stories!" or a black woman talking about my novel on the Tulsa Race Riot: "Oh, she gets a lot of things right, but there's a lot she doesn't know. You can't know it unless you've lived it." And, yes, I know this is true. I've witnessed only an inkling of the reality behind the words from an art poster I keep on my wall: "Native Is Pain—and You're Part?" I haven't lived that pain, and no amount of family storytelling about a Black Dutch-stands-for-Choctaw grandmother can change that. One cannot think or feel or believe one's way into being Indian. The longer I live here, the deeper my friendships with Indian people become, and the further the possible proofs of Native ancestry recede, the more I know this is true. Still, I cannot help where my heart lies.

When the doubting voices begin, I feel an urge to explain my complicated, contradictory sense of self, but to whom? And where? And how? No, I think. I'll just keep to my work, let others make their own assumptions. And so I hold my silence—even knowing that silence is a type of passing.

Interviewing James Brown, Tulsa Civic Center, January 28, 1969.
Left to right: Tom Ogans, David Lindemood, the author, unidentified student, Mr. Brown.
(Photo courtesy of Bartlesville High School; author's collection.)

Travis and Marlene with the author at her home in the Catskills, summer 1991.
(Author's collection.)

Marlene's family at their apartment on Lenox Avenue, Brooklyn, circa fall 2000.
Left to right: Travis, Errol, Marlene, and the author holding Ebony. *(Author's collection.)*

A WOUNDED PLACE

The wound is in me, as complex and deep in my flesh as blood and nerves. —WENDELL BERRY, *The Hidden Wound*

Oklahoma is a wounded place. The country as a whole is wounded, but my home state, birthed as it was in such profound hope and greed, violence and promise, is wounded in a particular way. From the Trail of Tears to the all-black towns to the rush of white settlement in the land runs, the coming together of black, white, and indigenous peoples in the old Indian Territory created a racial cauldron that boiled over in brutal ways large and small in the early part of the twentieth century. A hundred years later, we are still living out that legacy whether we know it or not. And most of us don't know it. Or let me say this: most white people don't know it.

Writing in the 1980s, Wendell Berry, that masterful American poet, writer, and thinker, called racism our nation's "hidden wound." I would qualify the phrase by saying, "hidden from white people." Americans of color surely haven't found racism to be hidden. But white America is, I believe, who Wendell Berry was addressing. It's who I'm writing to. I didn't know that for a long time. Didn't think about it, really. Much of my journey as a writer has been in coming to understand that this is so. I think in part it's because I came of age when I did, where I did, that I'm always looking to peel back the scabs, dig underneath the scars. I grew up in the 1960s not far from Tulsa never having heard a whisper about the racial pogrom that took place there in 1921. In this I'm no different from the majority of white people. The silence surrounding the Tulsa Race Riot was so absolute that I discovered the story only in young adulthood, and then only by accident.

But black people knew. The story of the riot was handed down orally in black families—not all families, but many, and not just in Oklahoma, but all over the country—in direct contradiction to the complicit silence in white communities. When I think of why the wounds of race won't heal in this country, I think of the fact that for decades blacks and whites lived and worked in close proximity to one another, with most black people knowing what happened in Tulsa in 1921 and most white people entirely ignorant of it. That's the nature of the chasm between us. That's the legacy we're still living out, not only in Oklahoma but all over the nation, just as we're living out our birth-rights of slavery and genocide and our homegrown brand of terrorism: massacres and lynchings. We're still living Wounded Knee and Jim Crow, still suffering the long hurt of the boarding schools, the theft of Indian children through forced adoptions. As a nation we're all living it, but it's only the dominant culture, the so-called normative culture, that doesn't recognize this.

The little city of Bartlesville, where I grew up, is situated on grassy rolling prairie some fifty miles north of Tulsa, just twenty miles south of the Kansas border. In the 1960s, B'ville, as we called it, was a lively, thriving company town, the headquarters for Phillips 66 Petroleum, a compact city of wealth and good living. We had excellent schools, clean streets, one of the highest per capita incomes in the nation—and an ugly race-and-class-based poverty that was kept strictly relegated to certain pockets of town. A decade past *Brown v. Board of Education*, the elementary schools in Bartlesville were still segregated. All the black children went to Douglass Elementary on the west side of town. No white child went there. Before I entered junior high, I had never sat next to or even spoken to a black person.

That was in 1963. The same year Bartlesville was named an All-America City by the National Civic League. The year President Kennedy was shot. The year the governor of Alabama stood on his capitol's steps declaring, "Segregation today, segregation tomorrow, segregation forever." The same year James Baldwin penned an open letter to his teenage nephew describing America as he saw it and lived it, telling his nephew how life would be for him as a young black man growing up here, the soul-killing injustices and daily devastations he'd be living through. The America Baldwin was writing about is the one I grew up in, a young white girl coming of age with all the privileges and presumptions of whiteness, and nobody telling me what that America truly was, or why it was that way. Nobody but James Baldwin, and we weren't reading him.

From seventh grade on, I rode a school bus every day through the section of Bartlesville that politer white folks called "colored town," past ragged streets and flimsy houses even more dilapidated than the worst of the houses belonging to poor whites. For six years, twice a day, nine months of the year—more than three thousand times—I rode through this area of oppressive poverty where no white person lived, though no black person in our town lived anywhere else, and not once did I question why this was so. I never thought about it. The border between whites and blacks was unquestioned, unarticulated, unassailable, and as invisible as gravity. How did I learn about it? I can't tell you. It was as if we took it in with the air we breathed. In this I doubt my experience was much different from that of other white kids growing up in the American South then—except Oklahoma is not the American South. It is, or was, Huck Finn's "Injun Territory": that elusive promise of freedom in the West that looms so large in our master narrative. It is, or was, in myriad ways, America's Promised Land.

By the time I entered high school, the civil rights movement was part of our daily current events, what we talked about in social studies. I grew to be quite sentimental about notions of social justice. Theoretically, I was all for the idea of integration, which to me meant blacks and whites going to school together. Not that I would have dreamed of becoming friends with any of the black kids who went to our high school but took separate buses to get there, ate at separate cafeteria tables. Certainly I thought black people ought to be allowed to vote, to eat at any lunch counter they wanted. But I couldn't have imagined getting off my school bus and walking through their streets, entering black people's homes, worshiping alongside them in their churches. I kept my transistor radio tuned to KAKC in Tulsa because they played all my favorite soul artists—Aretha Franklin, Sam and Dave, Otis Redding, James Brown—but I wouldn't have been caught dead hanging out with black kids any more than I would have been caught dead hanging out with the poorest whites. I thought the separation was as much about class as it was about race. Never once did it dawn on me that there was no such thing as a black middle class in our town, or anywhere else I'd ever been. If anyone had challenged me to think about it, I might have said that I thought black people were just naturally poor.

In 1969 the great soul singer James Brown came to Tulsa. I was a senior in high school then, a staff writer for our school newspaper, and I got assigned along with three other students to go to the Tulsa Civic Center to interview Brown after the concert. David Lindemood, a smart, hip white kid who was cool enough that we all called him by his last name, had lobbied our journalism teacher for the chance to interview his idol, the Hardest Working Man in Show Business, the King of Funk, the famously infamous Godfather of Soul. How he'd wrangled access to Mr. Brown I didn't know, but drive to Tulsa we did, one winter-dark evening in Lindemood's car, with me riding shotgun and two other staffers in the backseat: Tom Ogans, a quiet, well-liked black kid, and Steve Lively, an aptly named red-headed livewire and the school paper's primary photographer. We weren't scheduled to go to the concert itself, only backstage afterward for the interview. I wondered why we weren't seeing the show so we could write about that, too, but I didn't ask.

We arrived at the Civic Center just as the concert was letting out. The audience pouring from the concert hall was huge, loud, celebratory, and black. In those moments, my world turned around. I became untethered, disoriented. I could have been in another universe for how stunned and bewildered I felt. It wasn't just that I'd never been in the minority, it was that my adolescent mind was incapable of grasping such a thing even as I was in the middle of it. I felt like a flimsy white leaf tossed about on a sea of blackness.

It occurred to me that Lindemood had understood very well that ours would be three of very few white faces in that huge arena, and that was why he hadn't lobbied for us to go to the concert. I shrank down inside myself, baffled and timid, trying not to lose sight of his blond head as we made our way against the streaming crowd into the bowels of the Civic Center.

This was January 28, 1969. The assassination of Martin Luther King had taken place ten months before. U.S. athletes Tommie Smith and John Carlos had just rocked white America's sensibilities with their Black Power salute at the 1968 Olympics. James Brown's anthem "Say It Loud—I'm Black and I'm Proud" had been at the top of the charts for five months.

I remember how bright the dressing room seemed, all those lighted mirrors. Mr. Brown had just finished one of his stunningly athletic shows, but he was cool and relaxed as we filed in. We weren't the only students in the room; there were kids from other area schools, maybe seven or eight of us in all. Brown's campaign to encourage young people to stay in school was well established; he had set up a foundation to send black kids to college, he gave readily of his time to young people. For years I kept tucked away in my billfold the small scrap of notebook paper he signed for me that night: "Stay in school. James Brown."

The picture that appeared later in our school newspaper shows Lindemood and me sitting in metal folding chairs directly across from Brown. Behind us, Tom Ogans sits on the edge of a dressing table, smiling. Mr. Brown is clearly explaining something of significance. I wish I knew what was being said at that moment when Steve Lively snapped the picture, but I don't remember. What I do remember, with great chagrin, is this: I argued with James Brown.

I mean *argued*—disagreeing with him, contradicting him, jumping in with my own youthful opinions for what seems now, in memory, like an excruciatingly long time. I couldn't understand why the singer couldn't understand what I was trying to explain to him. "But we've got to have integration!" I kept saying. "How else are we going to get to know each other?"

And James Brown answered, essentially, no, that's not it.

I continued to press upon Mr. Brown my absolute confidence that all that was needed to fix our country's racial problems was for white kids and black kids to go to school together. "How will we ever get over our prejudices," I insisted, "if we don't know each other?" I hadn't a clue that "integration" and "desegregation" were not even the same thing. Never once did it occur to me that if we weren't so segregated in terms of jobs and opportunity and housing, if blacks and whites lived in the same neighborhoods and worshiped in the same churches and worked together in the same offices, the issue of school desegregation would be moot. I thought Mr. Brown was simply saying we didn't need integration at all.

What he was actually saying I can glean only in retrospect from the article that appeared in our school paper: "Opportunity is what we need. Sure I've made it. But I've made it as James Brown, not as a man. I want to be a man, not a singer. This is true with every black man in the United States."

I recall now grainy television images: African American men in suits and dark fedoras carrying signs in the streets of Memphis that read "I AM A MAN." Martin Luther King Jr. had gone to the Memphis garbage workers' strike to lend support to their economic justice campaign. That's what he was doing in Memphis when he was killed.

That cold January night in Tulsa, James Brown was trying to make me see that integration was a smokescreen—a necessary beginning, yes, certainly, but a lie unless accompanied by the whole change, because there can be no racial equality without economic parity, no social justice without economic justice. I see now the line of progression from Abraham Lincoln's question before emancipation, "Is the Negro a man?"; to King's assassination when black men were marching in Memphis declaring "I *Am* a Man"; to James Brown's black power anthem, "Say It Loud—I'm Black and I'm Proud." I couldn't hear the message in Brown's lyrics then, only that gritty shout of racial pride, but his message was clearly also about economic justice: "All the work I did was for the other man, and now we demand to do things for ourselves."

Why did the most massive white assault on a black community in our nation's history take place in Tulsa? Because Tulsa's Greenwood District was so wealthy. "The finest example of Negro self-sufficiency in the nation," W. E. B. Du Bois described it three months before it was destroyed. How did such wealth come to be created in the former Indian Territory? The answers are as complex and paradoxical as all of Oklahoma's story. One part is the strength and self-sufficiency of the Freedmen, who arrived here as slaves of mixed-blood Indians, were freed by force and enrolled in the tribes at the insistence of the federal government after the Civil War, and who had been living here in autonomy for decades by the time of statehood in 1907.* Another part is how so many African Americans fled to this Promised Land from the post-Reconstruction southern states. They came in hopes of freedom and economic opportunity, but also in reaction to the rise of the Ku Klux Klan and the proliferation of racial terrorism in the South. Many of these Exodusters became the prosperous professional class in thriving black communities here, the doctors and lawyers, newsmen and businessmen and entrepreneurs, and at the same time, poor and striving and entrepreneurial whites were also flocking here for many of the same economic and landless reasons: southern whites who re-created in the Territory the same racial climate of fear and subjuga- tion and intense segregation they'd had in Alabama and Mississippi— lines of separation so rigidly enforced that in places like Tulsa no black person was permitted to live outside the black district except inside servants' quarters in white homes. Paradoxically, one consequence of such intense segregation was the fact that the money made in the black community stayed in the black community, circulating and bringing prosperity to the people who lived there. So why did I grow up believing that black people were just naturally poor? Because the white obliteration of black wealth in Tulsa on May 31 and June 1, 1921, was absolute. Because the effects of the riot's terror and destruction rolled north to Bartlesville, rippling out in waves to black communities all across Oklahoma, and beyond.

Many times I've returned to the image of that young white girl in Tulsa insisting to James Brown, who'd grown up under America's particular brand of terrorism—lynchings, burnings, social and economic subjugation—that all we needed to solve our country's race problems was for white kids and black kids to go to school together. I see her arguing with the man; I can feel again my own certainty that I was right, and my red-faced mortification when Lindemood made a gesture for me to hush up. I'm detached from that girl now, and yet she is me. She is, in a sense, all of us. She's ignorant, yes, and rude, and

---

* A powerful testament to this is the autobiography of John Hope Franklin's father, B. C. Franklin, a Chickasaw freedman: *My Life and an Era: The Autobiography of Buck Colbert Franklin* (Baton Rouge: Louisiana State University Press, 1997).

stunningly naïve, but she's also innocent in a way that I wouldn't comprehend for years. Not, in fact, until I encountered that other James B. whose words would become so important to me, James Baldwin.

I was on a plane flying from Tulsa back to my home in Brooklyn in the fall of 1987 when I read James Baldwin for the first time. I had been living in New York seven years then, had moved there in 1980 with $600, the promise of a sublet in Hell's Kitchen, and an artist's hunger inside me. I'd thought acting on the stage would answer that ache, but it turned out to be writing. So that was one big change for me. Another was the gradual transformation in how I was coming to see race in this country. I don't know if that transformation would have happened—could have happened—if I'd stayed in Oklahoma. In his essay "Going to the Territory," Ralph Ellison surmises that it was because he grew up in Oklahoma that he became the writer he became. "Geography is fate," he said, evoking Heraclitus. I often think how true that has been for me. And not just geography, of course, but era. Had I not grown up in a time and place of such overt prejudice and segregation, so that the layers of white bias were integrated all through my being, and had I not moved to New York City, a place of such thorough melding of the races but with its own racial wounds continuously erupting, I would be a different person. Certainly I would be a different writer. Perhaps I would not be a writer at all.

Not that I was thinking about race or writing either one when I moved to New York City; I was just chasing that acting dream. But the early 1980s were years of high crime and racial tension in New York: it was the beginning of the devastating crack epidemic, and stories of violence and "black crime" spewed forth daily from the tabloids. In 1982 a black transit worker, Willie Turks, was dragged from his car and killed by a white mob in Gravesend, Brooklyn. In 1984 a white subway rider, Bernhard Goetz, shot five young black men he said were getting ready to rob him. Mayor Ed Koch exacerbated tensions with his blunt comments; racialized news stories dominated the headlines in the *New York Post* and *Daily News*. But except for how these stories elevated my sense of fear when I rode the subway or walked alone in my neighborhood at night, they simply washed over me. I ignored them or pushed them away. I didn't think they had anything to do with me.

By the time I read James Baldwin on that plane in '87, I was beginning to know better. My husband and I had moved from Manhattan to Brooklyn, I'd turned from acting to writing, I was pursuing an MFA degree in creative writing, and I had begun to teach comp classes at Brooklyn College, where the majority of my students were young people of color. I'd had a bit of an epiphany earlier that fall while standing in a Cobble Hill bookstore. I had gone there in search of a novel to give to one of my students, a young black man who seemed in danger of failing the required CUNY writing exam at the end of the semester. He was very bright but not yet an adequate writer, and he told me he hated to read. I thought if I could find a good story to engage him, maybe he would get excited about the written word and work harder on his papers. I stood in the crowded aisles of Community Bookstore on Court Street, turning in a slow circle, looking at all the shelves. What kind of book could I get for my student? Suddenly I was swept with an obvious and yet to me revolutionary understanding: none of these books would matter a whit to my student. They were all about *white* people.

We don't get many true epiphanies in our lives, but that's what this recognition felt like to me. A small shift in the universe. A new knowledge. A revelation. Why hadn't I ever thought of that before? Why had I never once considered what it must be like to live in a country where all the books, all the *stories*, are about the Other? It was an observation that was not precisely true, of course, though it would take me a while longer to know it. Still, in that moment I saw the world in a new way. I felt how the weight and wealth on those shelves—the weight of knowledge, of narrative, of worldview—was all from one culture: the white Anglo-Saxon Western European culture that had shaped my entire understanding of the world. For the first time, it didn't seem merely natural, the norm, but domineering, oppressive. For the first time, I grasped faintly what's meant by the "dominant" culture.

At last, over in one corner, I spied a shelf marked "Afro-American Literature," and on that segregated shelf I found Richard Wright's *Native Son*. I bought the book for my student. I don't know if he ever read it, but I did, before I gave it to him, and the book became both directly and indirectly the catalyst for an unfolding narrative that shapes my world and my work to this day. "The day *Native Son* appeared," the critic Irving Howe wrote in 1963, "American culture was changed forever." Can a novel still change a nation's culture? I don't know. I doubt it, not in our current fractured time. But a novel can change one person, and this one changed me. Wright's storytelling, his use of narrative voice and point of view, so captured me that, yes, I recognized the forces at work on Bigger Thomas, the weight of our violent, tortured race history, I understood intellectually where his violence comes from, why he kills, and then rapes and kills again, but more than that: I felt his same hatreds and fears, his powerlessness and rage—not abstractly but emotionally, inside myself. I found myself in deep, unwilling sympathy with him, rooting for his escape, hoping that in the end he might dodge the fate that America and his own nature have set out for him. That's the power of fiction, point of view, living inside a character's skin, and at the end, when I closed the book, I just wanted to know, why had I never read this before?

It's hard not to regret the poverty of my upbringing. I don't mean economic poverty, though my family was hardly well off, but the intellectual, spiritual, experiential poverty that caused me to see the world only through the prism of whiteness—or the reverse prism, I should say, because the lens doesn't refract white light into a spectrum of colors, but narrows and constricts the whole spectrum into one contracted white beam. Bartlesville was known for the excellence of its schools, and in these excellent schools we studied American and Oklahoma history, rigorous courses from which I carried away only a glossed-over partial truth about our state's and our nation's past. In our English classes we read *Silas Marner, Lord of the Flies, A Separate Peace*, but not *Invisible Man* or *Native Son* or *Black Elk Speaks*. We certainly did not read James Baldwin, neither his essays nor his fiction, and it wasn't until I began teaching that I encountered his work for the first time. That's one way reading Richard Wright changed my life: it was because of the lingering effects of *Native Son* that I brought with me on the plane that day a collection that included James Baldwin's story "Sonny's Blues," which is surely one of the finest pieces of American fiction ever written, and it is surely a measure of the poverty of my upbringing that it took me so long to find it. I still recall viscerally how the story gripped me—the language, the construction, the grief. By the time I reached the last line, "like the very cup of trembling," I was myself trembling, crying quietly, trying to hold the sound in. The words and that luminous image resonated in me, echoing, I realize now, my own church-saturated upbringing, though I didn't then understand why it touched me so hard. I just knew my soul was wrenched.

Within days I sought out Baldwin's other works, his novel *Go Tell It on the Mountain*, his essays in *Notes of a Native Son*. The country he showed me, and the rhythm and beauty of the language he delivered it in, shook me to my core. Then, in early December, I read in the *New York Times* that James Baldwin had died. I felt a kind of detached sadness combined with a self-centered sense of unfairness: I had just discovered Baldwin's work, hadn't even known he was still alive, and now he was gone. The obituary said he'd died of stomach cancer at his home in southern France; it analyzed his literary works, spoke of his "apocalyptic tone in prose," briefly summarized his life. There was a sidebar with the heading "In Baldwin's Own Words," a few lines of which read:

> The white man's unadmitted—and apparently, to him, unspeakable—private fears and longings are projected onto the Negro. The only way he can be released from the Negro's tyrannical power over him is to consent, in effect, to become black himself, to become a part of that suffering and dancing country.

I clipped that little square, a passage from "Down at the Cross: Letter from a Region in My Mind," and tacked it to my writing room bulletin board, where, yellowing and faded, it remained for two decades. I've put it away now for safekeeping, but the words remain etched in me. The last line in the obituary said that Baldwin's funeral was to be held on Tuesday at noon at the Cathedral of Saint John the Divine in Manhattan. I knew at once I would go.

Early on the morning of December 8, 1987, I took the subway from Brooklyn to Manhattan's Upper West Side and walked in brilliant winter sunlight with hundreds of others streaming from all directions toward the cathedral doorway. I was relieved to find that I was not the only white person there, though we were surely in the minority. As I mounted the steps, stood in line to find a seat, I tried to act as if I had a personal reason to be there, because I didn't want to seem like some kind of celebrity groupie come to see the famous people at the famous black writer's funeral. I edged slowly into the sanctuary, merged with the crowd of mourners, some five thousand of us (*so great a cloud of witnesses*, my mind said, silently quoting Hebrews), and was ushered into a tightly packed pew midway back. I thought of Baldwin's description of his father's funeral in "Notes of a Native Son," the vast distance from the paucity of that small gathering to this. I thought of how his mother hadn't been able to attend his father's funeral because she was confined with her last baby, Baldwin's youngest sister. I remembered how Baldwin described taking care of his brothers and sisters when they were little, and of course they would all be here on this day, and I wondered which of his brothers might have been the model for Sonny, thinking of how Sonny had taken his first toddling steps into his older brother's arms, blurring in my mind the parents and siblings in Baldwin's fiction with those in his autobiographical essays, even though as a fiction writer myself I knew better. I was lost in distracted musings about the interplay between a writer's life and art when the organ music began.

As the swell of the organ faded, there came a rhythmic pounding, a lone African drum, powerful, resonant, quickly joined by many drums, a solemn, thunderous, victorious salute as Baldwin's family and friends came down the aisle in ritual procession. From the front of the sanctuary there arose then the sacred sound of hymns, like the hymns of my growing-up years, but sung in a rich, soaring voice unlike any sound I'd ever heard in any church. It was the folksinger Odetta, her ringing voice like a choir and a prayer. When that sound faded, we heard Baldwin's own voice, a scratchy recording of him singing "Precious Lord, take my hand," his whispery baritone echoing in the vast space of the sanctuary, "Lead me on, let me stand," and it seemed I could almost hear my grandfather's tenor echoing behind it, "I am tired, I am weak, I am worn." That had been one of my Papaw Allie's favorite hymns. I felt a tightening of grief in my throat, as if I'd known the man, though I knew it wasn't really James Baldwin but my own grandfather that I mourned. It was then, after the music, that the tributes began.

This is what stays with me—not what the speakers said, for I remember very little of the specifics, except how they evoked

Baldwin's great gentleness and the raging fire in him that had never waned; but rather my response to their words, how uncomfortably I received them. When Maya Angelou and Amiri Baraka and Toni Morrison rose from their seats to talk about James Baldwin, they spoke with a kind of triumphant ferociousness that seemed to me both a celebration of Baldwin's fierceness and a condemnation of the America that produced the very fire and judgment in him for which he'd been at once so honored and so vilified. I listened to their voices lifted in anger and celebration, in triumph and condemnation, and found myself surprised and hurt to realize that, no, all is *not* forgiven, the past is *not* forgotten, the sins of my fathers have *not* been redeemed. But the country has changed! I wanted to cry out. *I've* changed. Can't we forget all that old stuff?

No, their voices seemed to answer. We cannot forget all that old stuff. Again and again they stood to talk about James Baldwin, celebrating that substance of truth which so shook me when I read his writings, but which I wished now to hear softened, ameliorated, muted in this time and place, for the soothing of my own spirit, that balm, that salve which I had, in fact, expected. I can see now a direct connection between the young white girl who argued with James Brown and the slightly older and wiser but no less white woman who sat in a pew hurt and mortified at James Baldwin's funeral. It's a through-line of the sort of innocence Baldwin described in his writings—not guiltless innocence, but a presumptuous, unwilled, and yet willing ignorance. In that 1963 letter to his nephew, written on the hundredth anniversary of Emancipation and collected in *The Fire Next Time*, Baldwin said:

> and this is the crime of which I accuse my country and my countrymen, and for which neither I nor time nor history will ever forgive them, that they have destroyed and are destroying hundreds of thousands of lives and do not know it and do not want to know it.

In my mind I hear a silent chorus of protests: "No, it isn't true! Or even if it once was, it's not like that anymore. And anyway, it's not *me. I* didn't do it." I know that feeling well: I've said it. I've lived it. This is what I was feeling that bright December day in the Cathedral of Saint John the Divine.

"But it is not permissible," Baldwin continued, "that the authors of devastation should also be innocent. It is the innocence which constitutes the crime."

The innocence which constitutes the crime.

A bit over a year and some later, I picked up a biography of Richard Wright by Margaret Walker, *Richard Wright: Daemonic Genius*, and it was there, on page 16, that I read that some of the worst race riots in this nation's history took place in the early 1920s in Atlanta, Georgia, in Elaine and West Helena, Arkansas—and in Tulsa, Oklahoma. I stared at those words: "Tulsa, Oklahoma." I felt as if I'd been gut-punched, like I'd found out some dark family secret, like someone had just said: Your parents are not your parents. You think you know who you are, but you don't know. In all the years I had lived both in and near Tulsa, I had never heard one word about a race riot there. I had never heard about any kind of race trouble in Oklahoma at all. Staring at the page, those few lines, choppy black letters on white paper, I had the sense of an essential missing piece—one I hadn't even known was absent—suddenly clicking into place. I knew at once that I would write about this. My mind ratcheted forward with thoughts of how I could ferret out the history, encase it in fiction, deck it with characters and intentions and sensory details . . . and all the while that sickening, bewildering feeling kept reeling in me, that sense of having been left out of something hugely important—of having been lied to. What else weren't they telling me? What else didn't I know?

Well, plenty, as it turns out.

That evening, I called my sister Ruth in Tulsa. She remembers our conversation vividly. It was winter, she says, probably late January or early February of 1989. She remembers standing barefoot astraddle the floor furnace in her house on South Olympia, holding the receiver to her ear, the long cord draped to the yellow wall phone in her dining room, talking to me in my kitchen in Brooklyn, the two of us linked across fifteen hundred miles by telephone wires. "Did you know there was a race riot in Tulsa?" I asked.

"Yes," she said. "I knew that."

"Wait a minute," I said, that sense of having been left out of the big stuff rising in me again. "We went to the same schools, we had all the same teachers. How come you knew about this and I didn't?"

"Vashti told me," she said.

Vashti was Ruth's husband's grandmother. She'd been a young girl living on the northern outskirts of Tulsa when it happened. Vashti hadn't seen the riot itself, but she had seen the aftermath, and some fifty years later, she told her granddaughter-in-law about it. Ruth described sitting in the living room in Vashti's tiny house on North Elgin, amidst her several poodles—this would have been the early 1970s, Ruth said, not long after she'd married into the family—listening to her describe how she had ridden in her father's flatbed wagon through the smoldering ruins of the black district. It was night, Vashti said, and they drove through smoke and charred timbers and crunching glass, stopping at last in a park on the east bank of the river. ("I think it must have been Newblock Park," Ruth said on the phone, "that little park over on Charles Page. It's not far from where I'm standing right now.") And this young white girl Vashti, an only child, probably no more than twelve or thirteen, sat in her father's wagon and looked at the bodies of black people lying about on the ground.

"My God," I said. "Was it that bad?"

"It was that bad. Vashti said there was a big bonfire on the riverbank, where they were burning the bodies."

"*Burning* them! Why didn't we learn about this in school? Our own grandma taught Oklahoma history, for heaven's sake! Looks like I would have heard *something*."

"People don't want to talk about it, Rilla. It was terrible, it was horrible; no one wants to admit something like that happened here."

"Well, I'm going to write about it," I said. "That's going to be my next book. My first novel. I'm going to come home and talk to Vashti and find out what happened."

But by the time I got back to Tulsa that summer to start the research, Ruth and her husband had separated, and soon after divorced, and I did not go to North Tulsa to visit with Vashti. Instead I set out for the Tulsa City-County Library armed with this snippet of oral history handed down from my sister's ex-husband's grandmother and the general date of the riot, early summer of 1921, and little else.

I went to the desk on the third floor and asked for directions to the newspaper microfilm files. Planting myself in front of the huge gray metal bank, I pulled out the heavy rolling drawer labeled *"Tulsa World, Tulsa Tribune, 1919–1938."* I pawed through the boxes of film and found the ones marked right up through April 1921, and the next ones beginning again in September, but the months surrounding the riot dates were missing. I went to the desk again, asked the woman sitting there if perhaps the boxes I needed had been checked out—maybe they were being read on the microfilm machine by another researcher right now?

"What dates are you looking for?"

"1921. Early summer."

"Ah, yes," she said, gazing up at me. "I think I know what you're wanting to look up. No, we don't have those microfilms here, not for the Tulsa papers. But I believe I can help you with what you want to know."

And so this knowledgeable and extremely helpful librarian showed me how to look up accounts of the riot in other periodicals of the era: the *New York Times*, the Los Angeles papers, the *Chicago Tribune*, *Crisis* magazine. We didn't talk about what had happened to the missing files. Years later I was told by a woman at an author event in Tulsa that the archives had been expunged before they reached the library; she said that the person at the newspaper office whose job it was to scan them onto microfilm had taken it upon herself or himself to save future generations from knowing the truth of our past. Whether that's so or not, I cannot say—I just know they weren't there when I began my research in the summer of 1989. I stayed in the library for hours, reading, because reference periodicals could not be checked out, and the more I read, the more stunned and sick I became. The scale of the Tulsa disaster was unprecedented, the numbers of dead, the miles of property destroyed: an epic assault by a mob of some ten thousand armed whites on the well-to-do black district called Greenwood, over a thousand homes and businesses looted and burned to the ground, hundreds killed and injured, the survivors rounded up and held in internment centers for weeks. The event was vast and shocking and by almost any measure one of the worst incidents of racial violence in the nation's history. I saw images of black men being herded at gunpoint through the streets by white men and boys. I saw dark smoke billowing, the smoldering aftermath: schools, churches, hospitals, newspaper offices, law offices, theaters, hotels, restaurants, all reduced to charred ashes. In the space of a few hours, one of the wealthiest, most vital black districts in America had been utterly destroyed. It would be as if a seventh of the white population of Manhattan had suddenly swept north into Harlem at the height of the Harlem Renaissance and burned it to the ground. The eruption in Tulsa was front-page news in every newspaper in the country. How could this have been covered up? I kept asking myself. How could I not know? How could any of us not know? James Baldwin's words echoed back to me:

[They] do not know it and do not want to know it.
It is the innocence which constitutes the crime.

Two months later I met Marlene. She was one of my students at Brooklyn College, fall semester, 1989. The second day of class, I asked the students to write down what most concerned them. "Don't sign your names," I said. "I want you to feel free to say whatever's on your mind. We're looking to generate writing topics here."

Race, I assumed, would be at the top of many of their lists. A couple of weeks before, on August 23, a black teenager and three friends had been surrounded by a mob of some thirty bat-wielding white kids in the Brooklyn neighborhood of Bensonhurst. One of the white kids pulled a gun and shot sixteen-year-old Yusef Hawkins dead. The Reverend Al Sharpton was then leading marches through Bensonhurst, where whites lined the streets, hoisting watermelons over their heads, shouting "Go home, niggers!" as the black marchers pressed forward, arms linked, chanting "No justice, no peace!" The media were in a feeding frenzy. You couldn't escape that racially charged story anywhere.

Marlene handed in a lined sheet of paper, ragged on one edge where it had been torn from a spiral notebook. The letters on the page were rounded, almost childlike, more printed than cursive, though a bit of a blend of both: "I can't tell my mother. I went to the clinic with my sister but I didn't stay, I got up and leave before I sign my name. I don't want to kill my baby."

I figured out who she was from her handwriting. She hadn't yet distinguished herself to me, just another pretty Jamaican girl in one of my classes, that soft lilt in her voice, a bit shy, perhaps. After the next class meeting, she lingered behind the others, gathering her books slowly, never quite glancing up. I met her at the door. "Marlene? Do you want to talk?" The relief in her face was like a wash of clean water. That's one of the few times I remember Marlene's emotions showing so plainly on her face.

We walked to the diner just off campus. I bought her lunch. Listened. Asked a few questions. Told her everything was going to be all right, but if she planned to keep her baby, she really had to tell her mother, that was all. And Marlene did tell her mother not long after, and everything, in those terms, at least, was just fine.

My students' papers, and their conversations, did center heavily on race. One of my classes—the one Marlene was in—was made up almost entirely of young people of color. My other class was mostly white students, many of them from Bensonhurst. The white young-sters knew with absolute certainty that the killing of Yusef Hawkins was never about race. It was about territory, they said. Those white kids in Bensonhurst weren't racists; they had black friends, even. They'd thought the black guys were in their neighborhood to beat up white kids, and anyway, the shooter was a lone wolf, a crazy kid; he didn't represent the real people in Bensonhurst, so why did that loudmouth Al Sharpton have to invade their neighborhood and stir everything up?

But the African American and West Indian students saw things with different eyes. I read it in their papers describing the thousand daily cuts and fears and indignities. They were telling me what James Baldwin told his nephew. They knew, with equal certainty, that Yusef Hawkins died because of the color of his skin. The differences in my classes illustrated more clearly than any statistics I might read: in this country, the way we witness the world, how we see, *what* we see, isn't determined by facts or objectivity but by the color of our own skin. A lot of white folks don't believe this, even when researchers tell us it is so. Or, to be more precise, we believe people from other cultures see things with biased eyes, their black or brown prejudice, whereas the facts in a given situation—the *truth*, we white people believe—is what we see.

Marlene finished the semester and then quit school while she waited for her baby to be born. I'd assumed she would drop away from my life as most students do. When she called just after the first of the year and asked me to be godmother to her unborn child, I was surprised and, frankly, a bit leery. I remember standing in my Carroll Gardens kitchen staring out at the wintry patio, the phone cord looped in a tangled spiral from the wall, the white receiver pressed to my ear, thinking, *Why me? Doesn't this girl have other friends or relatives who would be better to ask?* I had taken a particular interest in her during the semester, had brought her books on how to eat right, what to expect during her pregnancy, a few small baby items, but I knew her only as a former student, knew her family not at all. The idea of being connected to a family of another faith and culture whose American roots were set deeply in Brooklyn, when even then I knew it wasn't likely I would always live there—well, the idea seemed like a frightening obligation. I fumbled for words, finally blurted, "Let me think about it, okay?"

And I did think about it, talked it over with my husband, considered the notion from various angles. I suppose I came to the conclusion that "godmother" would be an honorary title, a passing commitment while the child was young. Certainly I had no recognition that our lives would be joined from that day forward when, the following morning, I called Marlene back and said yes.

The night I went to her baby shower was the first time I was ever inside a black home.

I remember leaving my mostly white neighborhood, driving deeper and deeper into the interior of Brooklyn until I reached unfamiliar streets, where every passerby, every car occupant, was black. I remember climbing their apartment house stairs with an overly friendly smile on my face. I remember the brightness of the kitchen, the spicy smells of cooking, the formality with which Marlene's mother welcomed me and led me to the living room, offered me a drink. I'd arrived too early. There were no other guests yet, just a friend taping baby blue streamers to the ceiling. I remember how out of place I felt, sipping my drink alone on the couch while the getting-ready activities swirled around me. The living room seemed dark, lit only by diffused light spilling from the kitchen, where the aromas of curried goat and stewed peas mingled with broiled bluefish, Jamaican spices, black cake. There were cheese puffs and potato chips set out on pastel-colored paper plates on the large coffee table, the low throb of reggae pounding from stereo speakers. Clear plastic sheathing on the white brocade sofa. Souvenir plaques from Jamaica on the walls. A gilt-framed tribute to *Mother* embossed with red roses. A stylized rendering of a black man and woman in African dress.

As other guests arrived, the living room began to fill with the rippling sound of patois gliding over the stutter of steel drums, the syncopated monotony of reggae rhythm. They were mostly women—relatives, family friends, a couple of Marlene's girlfriends from high school—but there were men, too, her brothers and their friends stopping by to pick up a Heineken or a wine cooler, to load up their plates from the mountains of food in the kitchen. When Marlene arrived, very late, for the surprise party that was clearly not much of a surprise, I thought I sensed something guarded in her, closed down, protective, though I couldn't tell what. She was much farther along in her pregnancy, of course, than when I'd last seen her at semester's end, very large and beautiful, her hair smoothed into a neatly rolled coif, her features muted, subdued, in the darkened room. At some point her boyfriend came in, the father of her baby, but I don't have a clear recollection of him. To me, he was indistinguishable from the other men passing through the living room in their high-top fade haircuts or Jheri curls and Kangol caps. Marlene sat quietly beneath a crepe paper parasol, smiling self-consciously from time to time at all the attention, but she said very little, her face holding a secret I didn't understand. That night was the first time I became aware of how Marlene's calm surface can belie oceans of feeling roiling underneath.

Travis was born on a cold February morning, the same week Nelson Mandela walked out of a South African prison after twenty-six years. New York's first black mayor, David Dinkins, elected in the aftermath of the Yusef Hawkins killing, had been in office six weeks. A Haitian woman had recently been beaten by a Korean store clerk on Church Avenue in Brooklyn, or she'd fallen down shrieking, pretending to be beaten, when the clerk accused her of shoplifting: two different versions. The boycott of Korean grocers by the black community in the West Indian district was in full swing. Every day, it seemed, a new headline blazed with the controversy. Tensions did not cut along black and white lines but between West Indian and Asian communities, and the public chatter was about culture, manners, ways of behavior—and economics. Always that.

As for my godson, I completely adored him. Every week I would drive across the borough to pick him up to come stay the night. In Marlene's neighborhood, I had to park far from their door and walk several blocks with Travis in my arms, and along those blocks there would be many people, all of them black, and inside the building there would be many people, all of them black, and this beautiful baby I was carrying in my arms was black, and the people glanced at us with curiosity, but they didn't stare. Still, the exposed skin on my face and hands felt drawn and hot, stinging, a fire of whiteness, a burning Caucasian husk.

Inside their apartment, I didn't feel that way. Inside, there was no color difference between them and me, in the same way there was no difference between Travis and my husband and me when he stayed with us—except on the street when a white passerby, usually female, would glance casually from my face to the baby's. At once she'd dash a quick bright smile that said something like *Oh, pardon me, I didn't mean to stare . . . well, my, aren't you just the cutest thing?* I'd push Travis in his stroller to nearby Carroll Park; we'd stop on the sidewalk in front of the big mirror behind a flower display at the deli on the corner and make faces at our reflections, and Travis would laugh and laugh, until soon all the passersby on the street and even the cashier inside the store would be laughing. In the park I would be the only white woman with a black child, though there would usually be several black women with white children—nannies, caretakers, who eyed me, I thought, with resentment, suspicion. *What's this white lady doing with this precious black child?* Or so my acute race consciousness told me. The city still roiled with place names signifying race trouble: Bensonhurst, Howard Beach, Central Park, Crown Heights. Every racial incident felt acute and personal to me. Complicated. Unresolvable. Guilt-filled.

When Travis was two, the L.A. riots broke out. I longed to drive across town to be with him and Marlene and their family. I wanted to say to them in an erupting world: It's not *me*. Not us. But I had a fever, a viral infection, and I was too sick to go. Through four wrenching days and nights, too ill to leave my apartment, I watched the news: the fires raging, the images of people running. A white man being pulled from his truck by black rioters and beaten, the talking heads giving their fatuous interpretations. The sad, helpless moment when Rodney King stood in front of all those microphones, saying, "Can we all get along?" I watched again and again the videotape of the white cops standing over him, a struggling black man on the pavement, beating him mercilessly, the image repeated on endless news loops. My sense of powerlessness, hopelessness, was profound. Los Angeles was so far away. The exact opposite side of the country. I had nothing to do with it, there was nothing I could do about it, and yet I felt responsible somehow.

It was a month later that my husband and I moved from our Brooklyn apartment to our cabin in the Catskill Mountains. Getting Travis now meant a six-hour drive round trip, so he came once a month instead of weekly, and he stayed with us for three or four days at a time instead of overnight. Our community upstate was whiter than ever. Not by choice. It's just where we lived.

Marlene still lived at home in Brooklyn with her mother and siblings. She was back in school, doing well, but I knew now the source of that guarded look I'd seen at her baby shower. Travis's father had become violent toward her, controlling, abusive. She had filed for an order of protection, had considered going into a shelter for battered women, but in the end she'd told him that it was finished, and something in her face, her demeanor, made him believe it. He let her go. For a while he still came around to see Travis, but the visits grew infrequent, and finally stopped altogether.

A few times when we got Travis for the weekend, Marlene came along, too. I remember sitting with her in a pizzeria in Monticello one day, watching Travis play peekaboo with two white ladies in a nearby booth. He was such a beautiful child, sweet natured, affectionate, with cocoa-colored skin and a thousand-watt smile. Every white woman who saw him fell in love with him. "What a little doll!" these ladies cooed. "Isn't he adorable?" I told Marlene how I dreaded the day he would run up against some white person's prejudice. "His feelings are going to be hurt," I said. "He won't know it's about history, he'll think it's about him, because so far in his young life every white person he's ever met has adored him." Marlene nodded, her face closed. There's always been that about her: how she holds her emotions so tightly, her expression calm and placid, revealing nothing, but the layers of feeling are palpable, just there below the surface. Sometimes the more closed her expression, the deeper the feeling. That day her face seemed to say I was talking about things I didn't really understand.

And I didn't, not then. On many levels I still don't. It's taken decades of being a part of Marlene's family, of being witness to the America that Baldwin was writing about to his fourteen-year-old nephew in 1963, that Ta-Nehisi Coates would still be describing for his fourteen-year-old son in 2015, to even begin to know how much I don't know. That's the challenge of living inside the prism of whiteness. Our skin and education and experience impart such privilege that we can't see it any more clearly than we see the gravity that pins us to the earth or the oxygen we breathe. I loved my toddler godson, loved Marlene and her family; I'd begun to have a faint inkling of what it means to live in America in brown skin, but I also lived in a very white, very liberal world, where my friends and acquaintances shared with me an unnamed faith that the promise of America, as Ralph Ellison wrote about it, was a true thing; that the arc of the moral universe was bending toward justice, as Martin Luther King had said; that the post-racial world we dreamed of was just over the horizon. The layers of presumption I'd grown up with, and lived under still, gave me eyes that are like the blind eyes of Mrs. Dalton in *Native Son*. I couldn't see the truth of the lie we live under in this country every day, couldn't recognize how the presumptions of whiteness shaped everything I thought and believed. I couldn't know, that day in the pizzeria, how very hard those presumptions would be to overcome.

All through Travis's young years, I continued researching and writing about the Tulsa Race Riot. Marlene's quiet affect became Graceful's in the novel, her worries and fears translated into the atmosphere of violence and segregation in 1920s Oklahoma. Setting out to write that book, I knew that I didn't want the white characters to be the Great White Savior heroes, like Atticus Finch in *To Kill a Mockingbird*, but rather the perpetrators, in large and small ways, of that apocalyptic destruction—the authors of devastation, in Baldwin's words. The work would take eleven years. When *Fire in Beulah* finally came out, we would be living in a new century, I'd have published a different first novel, *The Mercy Seat*, and I would know about America's racial past and its present in ways I couldn't have begun to know that day in the pizzeria when Trav was an adored and adorable toddler boy.

By the time Travis was an adolescent, big for his age, very grown looking though he was still just a kid, I'd begun to see. Of course it wasn't middle-aged, middle-class white women giving my godson grief. It was the white security guard at his middle school, for instance, who found Travis wearing his cap indoors one day in violation of school rules. The guard tried to confiscate it, but Travis resisted—that Yankees cap was a gift from his stepdad, Errol. Travis was six when Marlene married Errol, a recent immigrant from Jamaica, a good man, a hard worker, crazy about her, and—just as important—crazy about her son. Travis was equally crazy about Errol, and the fact that the Yankees cap was a gift from him made it all the more special. Travis was afraid he wouldn't get it back if the guard took it, so he held on. The guard grabbed him in a headlock, clamping his arm around my godson's throat, choking him, and Travis, unable to breathe, grabbed hold of the man's arm, trying to break free. The guard shoved him against the wall, jerked his hands behind him, and handcuffed him. Then he took Travis not to the principal's office for wearing a ball cap in school, but downtown to Brooklyn Central Booking, where my godson was charged with assaulting a school security officer. Travis was fourteen years old.

When he was old enough to drive, Marlene and Errol bought him a car. They were doing well by then, both advancing in their careers; they owned a home near the Belt Parkway, had two beautiful daughters in addition to Travis. A growing, happy middle-class family. Almost daily, Travis got stopped by the police while driving home from school. They'd always search his car, after asking his permission, which Travis always gave, in part because he knew he had nothing to hide, in part because he was afraid of what would happen if he refused. After the search, the police would issue a ticket for whatever excuse they'd used to stop him: failure to keep right, failure to use a turn signal. Garbage tickets, Marlene called them as she wrote out the checks to pay the fines.

When he was seventeen, Travis was arrested and jailed on a charge of petit larceny: seventy dollars' worth of accessory lights stripped off a car by three black youths who fled in a car that matched the description of his car. We knew he didn't do this thing, and not just because we know he's no thief: he was with Marlene in the dentist's office at the time printed on the complaint. She and I had talked on the phone then, and Trav was in the dentist's chair; we had the phone records, could get the dentist's sign-in sheet to prove it. It didn't make any difference. Once the detectives had settled on him, there was no stopping the process. They put him in a lineup in the late afternoon, for instance.

"A *lineup*?" an upstate lawyer friend of mine would later marvel. "For petit larceny?"

Yes, a lineup, with four other black males, all cops in street clothes, all above the age of thirty, Travis the only youth with braids in the room. Who was the complainant going to pick out but him? We'd been at the precinct since early in the day, but they didn't set that lineup until way late in the afternoon, so that Travis couldn't possibly be arraigned before the next morning. They intended for him to spend the night in Brooklyn Central Booking. They had a legitimizing phrase for what they were doing, though: this was "an uncooperative family."

Because just the day before, three armed white plainclothes detectives had stormed up Marlene's stairs, bursting in through her unlocked apartment door like it was a major drug bust instead of an effort to question a teenage boy about a possible case of petit larceny. They flashed their IDs; one of the detectives moved in close into Marlene's space, forcing her to step back, his voice loud and aggressive: "Where's your boyfriend?"

Marlene's hackles went up. "I don't have a *boyfriend*," she said. "I have a husband. He's at work now. What do you want?"

"Is this your son?" The detective waved an enlarged scan of Travis's driver's license photo. She didn't know what this was about, but she knew they had been there before, the previous week, rifling through her mailbox—a neighbor had told her. She was alone in the apartment now. Errol was working; their little girls, Ebony and Essence, were at day camp; Travis was out somewhere with his friends, savoring the end of summer. The detectives pressed deeper into the inside hall, looking all around the kitchen, toward the living room, up the stairs, all directions at once—like they wanted to swarm the whole apartment, Marlene said when she told me the story. She walked away, toward the sink, she said, because of how they were crowding her, and as she moved, a few words escaped, unwilled, based in long, hard experience. Under her breath she murmured, "I don't like cops."

"What! What did you say!" The detectives were nearly apoplectic. Words rained down on her; they'd make her sorry that she didn't *like* cops: "Bring your son down to the precinct for a lineup tomorrow, or we'll put out a warrant for his arrest."

"If you don't have a warrant right now," Marlene said, "you don't have any reason to be here. Get out of my house."

They left, but those muttered words were set to fall hard on her son. She called me that evening and told me what had happened, about their threat, that she and Errol were going to have to take Travis to the precinct. Next morning, I drove to Brooklyn. Marlene and Errol took time off from work, and we went with Travis to the station, tried to do everything properly. We told the investigating detective that Travis couldn't have done this thing, he was in the dentist's office at that time on that date. "If you want to go to trial," the detective said, "you can tell it to the judge." He was enormously polite to me, though, almost obsequious. He talked to me in friendly little asides, as if he and I were partners in some way—partners, I supposed he thought, in our whiteness. I don't know who he thought I was, a social worker, maybe, or Travis's teacher. He tried to act like this was all out of his hands, like he would let Travis go if he could. Still, he put Travis in that lineup way late in the day with older grown men and arrested him, and after that, we weren't allowed to see him.

The detective told us to go on home, there was nothing for us to do now; we could drive downtown tomorrow morning and get our boy. Errol left to pick up the girls and take them home for supper, but Marlene and I stayed. We stood for hours in the fluorescent-lit precinct lobby, waiting for the detective to bring Travis downstairs. We leaned against the wall—there was nowhere to sit—and watched the male and female officers gossiping at the front desk. Two angry, exhausted moms, one black and one white, our legs growing weary; we were hungry, thirsty. We talked.

She told me things she hadn't told me before—not because she hadn't wanted to worry me, she said, but because it was just normal. Just what you had to put up with. How since Travis had gotten his car for his birthday, he'd been stopped by the police and hassled again and again. I knew all about Driving While Black, but still the facts seemed incredible to me then: how the two patrolmen assigned to Travis's high school for security would follow him in the afternoons, cruising along slowly behind him while he walked to his car, and when he pulled out, they'd follow, sometimes a few blocks, sometimes several miles, before they turned on their patrol lights. They'd make him get out and stand beside the car while they searched it. The side panels in the car doors were loose now from all their searches, the glove box lock busted. They never found anything to arrest him for, of course, but they kept trying, because apparently in their view there was no way a black teenager should be driving a late model car unless he was a drug dealer. "You don't even know how much money I spent on those tickets. Sometimes you just get mad and don't want to pay it."

"That's it," I said. "That's why they zeroed in on Travis. All those tickets they issued, they'd have the make of the car on them. Travis's car is the same as that car on the complaint."

Marlene nodded. Of course. That made sense.

I said, "Maybe he shouldn't drive to school."

"What?" she said. "I'm going to buy him a car and then let it sit in the driveway while he takes public transportation?" She looked at me very evenly. "If he was white and had a car, you suppose it would be against the law for him to drive it to school? You suppose his parents would make him leave it home so he wouldn't be hassled?"

There it was, the truth smacking me again, as it has hit me so many times in the two decades since Marlene and her family became my family, too. For a flickering instant, my white mind presumed that the solution would be for Travis to bend to racial profiling by trying to avoid it. It took a moment, and Marlene's steady gaze, before it occurred to me to ask myself, Why can't my godson drive a nice car to school? Why can't he dress the way he wants to?

I was still asking myself those questions a couple of hours later when they brought Travis downstairs in handcuffs and put him in a barred holding tank on the far side of the lobby along with three other black men waiting to be bused downtown. Travis wouldn't look at us. His mother and I stood across the room hoping to tell him with our eyes that we were there for him, but Travis kept his head down, his gaze on the dirty tile floor. We left only after they'd herded him and the others in handcuffs outside to the van. Then, truly, there was nothing left for us to do. And so we went home, to Marlene's house; she fed the girls supper, and, very late, we went to bed. But neither she nor I slept. We both stayed awake the whole night, waiting for daylight so we could go downtown and get him.

Early next morning we took a cab to the Brooklyn courthouse, where we sat with other families, all of them black, and watched our boy brought in once more in handcuffs. Travis had stayed awake all night, too, he later told us: sitting on a bench in a filthy jail cell watching a naked man raving out of his head and another urinating on the floor; the overcrowding and stench were so bad, he said, that he sat up the whole night with his back to the wall, would not touch the rank bologna sandwich he was offered, or drink the water. He was given a court date, released to the attorney Marlene and Errol had hired. That lawyer turned out to be as uninterested in the fact that Travis was innocent as the detectives had been—his only concern seemed to be collecting his fee each time we went back to court, which happened four different times, spread out over several months. They fired the first lawyer, hired a different one. The arrest cost them thousands of dollars, much lost time at work, a missed tenth wedding anniversary vacation. What it cost Travis is hard to say.

In the end he pled guilty to a crime he didn't commit because the new lawyer said it was the only way to guarantee he wouldn't have a record. Travis was planning on college the next year; he'd be looking for work; a police record would dog him all through the bright future we hoped for him. Maybe the charges would be dismissed if he went to trial, but maybe not, and in any case a trial would cost the family even more money. And so it was agreed that the lawyer would arrange for a guilty plea and restitution for the seventy-dollar lights in exchange for the record being expunged if Travis "stayed out of trouble" for the next six months. I want to tell you something: it is nearly impossible for a young black man to stay out of trouble in a country where skin color is the marker for suspicion and violence and grief.

Travis is grown now, the father of a little girl. The police still stop him on the street, search him, search his car. He knows to stand motionless, keep his hands where the cops can see them, be cooperative, polite. He knows, but still I worry. As he moved out of his teen years, he gradually quit coming upstate to visit so much. His younger sisters started coming instead, Ebony and Essence, my goddaughters, beautiful, smart, funny, laughing girls. They were quite young when we began our tradition of their staying with us in the Catskills for a week around the Fourth of July. The summer of 2013, though, Marlene delayed our plans. I could tell from her emails there was something going on. She was distracted, busy at work, she said, but I sensed it was more than that. But I thought it couldn't be anything too troublesome or she would have called to talk. We finally set the date for me to come pick up the girls. Marlene told me she wouldn't be going to work that day, she had something she had to do. "What's going on?" I asked her.

"I'll tell you this evening," she said. "I don't want to talk about it on the phone."

Marlene was upstairs when I got there. Errol was in the kitchen with the girls, getting ready to leave for his softball game. He plays in a summer league, is a terrific player, always wins trophies, and usually when he heads out to a game, he's joking, high spirited, teasing his daughters. This evening, though, he was very quiet. I could sense a kind of, I don't know . . . a darkness in him. A weight I'd never seen before. Marlene, too, when she came downstairs, was more silent than usual. They had that air of grownups trying to make things seem normal in front of the kids. Travis wasn't around. The girls, for their part, seemed fine, though, just their normal happy selves. I had a tight feeling in my chest. "Where's Travis?" I said, half afraid to ask. "Oh, he's at school," Marlene said. "He has a night class." Okay. If not Travis, then who? What? I remembered then that Errol's younger brother was visiting from Jamaica. I was afraid it might have to do with him, because Errol was the one enveloped in a dark cloud.

After Errol left, Marlene sent the girls upstairs so we could talk. We have a kind of ritual, she and I, when we tell each other important stories. We'll sit alone in her living room, she in the armchair, me on the side sofa, one speaking, the other listening. When she came home from Jamaica after her nephew was killed there, we sat just this way as she told me the story, how Delroy died in a field outside Kingston, the fear on the boy's face even in death. After my sister-in-law died from cancer in Boston, I drove to Brooklyn, and we sat this way while I told Marlene about holding Dibbie's hand as she drew her last breath. Marlene's father's final illness, what she said to him the last time she saw him, his funeral. My niece's troubles in Oklahoma when her husband was deported. Family stories. The big stuff.

Marlene went to a closet and brought out a brown paper bag stuffed with clothing; she sat in her chair, pulled out different items, spread them formally on the living room floor: a man's dark vest, ripped into two pieces; a red shirt, torn and bloodstained; torn men's khaki trousers, also bloodstained. She laid out a woman's dressy outfit, too, a summery short skirt and pretty blouse—her own clothes—but it was the bloodstained man's shirt and trousers that caused my heart to catch. The shiny black vest ripped into two pieces. Inert evidence of violence, eloquent, silent.

"It was a beautiful night," Marlene began. "A holiday weekend. Me and Errol just sitting home, relaxing. Travis and his girlfriend went out, and around midnight he called . . ."

Travis told her it was a fine evening at the nightclub where they'd gone to celebrate the beginning of summer: good Jamaican food, good music; some of their friends were there. He wanted Marlene and Errol to come out. So they dressed up nice and drove over to Flatbush. They had just gotten settled at a table and ordered a drink when the overhead lights came on, the music stopped, and everybody was ordered to leave.

Once they got outside, they saw a man lying on the sidewalk, people milling around the front of the club saying he'd been shot; there were sirens, a lot of turmoil. No one wants to be around a shooting, Marlene said, an investigation, police trouble. Travis and his girlfriend hurried to his car parked on the street and left. Marlene and Errol walked quickly to the club lot where they'd parked their Lexus. They passed a woman lying on the sidewalk near the entrance to the parking lot. They hurried on, got in the Lexus, and Errol started to pull out, had moved maybe half a car length, when they heard a voice yelling, "Stop! Get out of the car!"

It took them a second to realize it was a police officer, and that he was yelling at them. Errol stopped, put the car in park, rolled down the window to find out what he wanted, but the cop was still yelling, "Get out of the car! Get out of the car!" "Okay, man," Errol said. "Hold on, give me a second." He started to glide the window back up to get out of the car, and at once the cop began to beat his gun butt on the window. "Get out of the car! Get out of the car!" Before Errol could open the door, the cop smashed the window, glass shattering all over the front seat, and then he reached in, jerked open the door, dragged Errol out onto the ground. By then other cops were swarming; a female officer was on the passenger side telling Marlene to get out of the car. The first cop had Errol handcuffed already. He wrenched him up off the pavement and shoved him against the Lexus, and Errol stumbled, off balance with his hands cuffed behind him, and the cops, all together and at once, piled on Errol and began to beat him.

"They beat him and beat him," Marlene said. "They take him between two cars so nobody can see, and they beat my husband and I can't do anything. The woman cop was there beside me by my side of the car. I'm yelling, 'What are you doing? You just going to kill him for no reason?' They have their guns drawn, they beat him with batons, with flashlights, it's dark, there are so many cops on him, and I'm just watching my husband get beaten, I can't do anything. His hands are cuffed behind him, his head over a guardrail, they're beating him all over his back, his legs, his head, I can hear the grunts and thuds, hear those batons smashing down on the steel guardrail, and it just goes on and on and on. Nobody stopping them. Nobody to stop them. They beat Errol till his pants are down to his knees, they rip his clothes." She touched the two halves of the vest. "His belt broke, they tore off the chain around his throat where he keeps his wedding ring. That ring just lost now, we'll never find it. They beat his head horribly, but they don't beat his face. They don't want anyone to see it. I finally think to cry out, 'I hope somebody videoing this! Somebody video this! You see what they're doing?' That, finally, is when the beating stop. That is the only thing that stop them. I think now if I didn't yell that, maybe they really would have killed my husband."

She paused. I stared at the torn clothing. When Marlene went on, her voice was low and quiet. "I'm just glad Travis left already. I think if he was there he would have jumped in. I know they would have killed him." She looked at me. "Isn't that something? The one thing I have to be grateful for is my son wasn't there to see his father beat like that, because otherwise I think he would be dead. They would maybe both be."

Listening, my throat tight, my heart racing, I felt a dark fire in my chest, familiar to me now after all these years: hatred, and outrage, and fury. I was crying, too, more or less, a dry weeping that stopped at my throat, my anger so great I couldn't make any tears. When I was able to speak finally, I didn't ask why—why would the police do that to a man like Errol, a hardworking family man, a loving father, a law-abiding citizen who has never in his life been arrested, never once lifted a violent hand to anyone? I asked only, "How many were there?"

"I don't know," Marlene said. "Maybe seven or eight doing the beating. Others all over the parking area, the woman cop by me."

"Were they all white?"

"The ones that was beating him, yes."

"Why didn't you tell me?" The beating had happened in late May. This was August. They had been dealing with the aftermath all summer. "I don't know," she said. "You were in Oklahoma when it happened. They had those tornados down there, you had your family to think about. I didn't want to worry you . . ." She grew quiet, shook her head. "I didn't want to talk about it on the phone." We sat in silence a while. I could hear the girls giggling upstairs, their TV music shows going. In a few minutes, Marlene went on to tell me the rest of the story.

She and Errol were both arrested, put in the back of a cruiser with their hands cuffed, taken down to Brooklyn Central Booking, locked up in holding cells. "You cannot believe how filthy that place is," she told me. "How disgusting. How terrible it smells." Marlene's face, when she told me this part, held all the layers of pain and indignity.

I could see what it had cost her, being put in that degrading place. They charged her with two misdemeanors: Obstructing Government Administration, Failure to Obey Police Officer. She asked for a desk appearance ticket, a summons, so she could go home to her children, but the officer said no, she had to wait and see the judge. And so my godson's mother, a successful professional woman, a kind and graceful law-abiding person, sat in a filthy cell in Central Booking all night and all day and most of the next night. In the end they released her after 1:00 A.M. onto the dark streets of downtown Brooklyn, alone, with no money, no purse, no phone, no way to go home or to call anyone to come get her. No way to know what they had done with her husband.

Errol, horribly beaten as he was, they held for two days. They'd given him a Breathalyzer test as soon as they brought him in, and when it came back negative, they drove him to a second location for a more detailed drug test. They wanted him to be drunk or on drugs. They needed a reason, a justification. They knew they had made a mistake. They charged him with reckless endangerment, resisting arrest, a long list of charges. The officer who handled the paperwork came in to talk to him: "You know I didn't have anything to do with this, right?" he said. Meaning the beating. He told Errol he shouldn't go to the hospital now, not from the precinct; it would just make everything take longer. "Wait to get released," the cop said, "and then go for medical attention if you need it."

And Errol did need medical care. He went to the emergency room three times over the next few weeks. The headaches wouldn't stop. His hand was numb, he couldn't feel his thumb; he could move it but couldn't feel it. Every time he breathed, he felt pains all through his torso—fractured ribs. When he went to the hospital the first time, on the day he was finally released, the attending physician asked him what had happened to him. He told her. She said he should file a report. She called the precinct, and they said they would send someone to take Errol's statement. He waited at the hospital for hours. No one from the precinct came. The physician had to go off duty. "I'm sorry," she told him. Errol nodded, said thanks for trying, and he drove himself home in his car with its busted window. But that was after he'd spent two days in a filthy holding cell. He was never allowed to make his call.

Marlene had finally gotten a ride home from a gypsy cab driver—an East Indian man with a heart, she said; he had spotted her walking on the dark predawn street and stopped, and when she told him she had no money but would pay him when she got home, the man drove her all the way across the borough to their apartment. Over the next two days, Marlene called friends and family until she found a lawyer; she took thousands of dollars from savings to pay his retainer and the bond he arranged to get Errol out of jail. Thousands more for him to represent Errol to get the felony charges against him reduced. Not to defend him. Not to say this man is innocent, but to arrange for a plea deal. If Errol was convicted of a felony, he could go to prison; he could lose his job, his means of supporting his family.

Marlene told me his court date had been that very morning. This was why she had taken the day off from work. Errol was furious in that courtroom, she said. She'd been afraid for him, what the anger might do. "Where's all the white kids?" he'd kept saying. "Don't any white kids commit crimes in Brooklyn?" Every defendant was black or Latino. The only whites in the room were people who worked there: lawyers, clerks, district attorneys, judges. As the lawyer had arranged, Errol pled guilty to a misdemeanor charge of disorderly conduct and received a sentence of three days of community service and court costs. The charges against Marlene had been dropped. This was the source of the dark weight I had felt when I came in the kitchen: Errol's anger, frustration, outrage, all held tightly contained inside him, along with the overwhelming sense of the injustice, and his own powerlessness in the face of it.

He felt he'd had no choice. The arrests had already cost them upwards of ten thousand dollars for lawyers' fees, bail, medical bills, repairs to his car. They didn't have the thousands more it would cost to go to trial and claim his innocence. And if they did go to trial, as the lawyer pointed out, there was no guarantee Errol wouldn't be convicted. It would be Errol's word against the word of the police. The lawyer had tried to get the videotape from the parking lot security camera showing the beating, but the police had already confiscated it by the time he went to the club to ask.

And so, just like Travis before him, Errol pled guilty to a crime he didn't commit. Errol is a master technician for a cable company.

Marlene is an associate dean for a major university in Manhattan. Neither had ever been in any trouble with police, ever had so much as a traffic ticket. There was no reason this should have happened to them. Except it did.

I see my godson's smile like honeyed lightning when he was a little boy, and I see him as a teenager in braids and handcuffs inside a steel cage in the lobby of a Brooklyn precinct, where they held him for hours before taking him downtown to book him for a crime he did not commit. I see my godson's father teasing his giggling daughters, leaving for his ball games, coming home tired from work. I see him struggling on the ground, powerless, his hands cuffed behind him, trying to avoid the blows from police batons, and Marlene crying out from the other side of their car, helpless, and the beating going on and on and on. Not in 1963 in the old slaveholding South, not in 1992 in a ghetto in Los Angeles, but in 2013 in a dark parking lot in Brooklyn.

This was a year before the death of Eric Garner on Staten Island at the hands of the NYPD. A year before the unleashing of video evidence—cascading evidence, video after video after video, visceral and violent—would force white Americans of good heart and goodwill to a kind of reckoning. Say a place name, and the wound that goes with it comes to mind: Ferguson, Missouri. Staten Island. Baltimore. Cleveland. Charleston. We have people's names to go with those place names: Michael Brown. Eric Garner. Freddie Gray. Tamir Rice. Walter Scott. But how long will we know their names? How many now remember the name of Yusef Hawkins, who was killed by a white mob in Bensonhurst in 1989? From the violence that erupted in Tulsa in 1921, we don't have names; we don't even have precise numbers. Why is that? One thing we ought not forget in this America is how our impulse to forget is so strong.

Two years later, on July 13, 2015, in the midst of a continuing onslaught of stories about racial violence taking place all over America, I drove to Brooklyn to pick up the girls to come stay with us for their summer week in the Catskills. We had missed our annual Fourth of July visit again—not because Marlene had postponed this time, but because my husband and I had been in Oklahoma over the weekend of the fourth, making preparations to move here full time. And the girls were growing up—young teenagers now, and already taller than me—and I didn't know how many more summers I'd have them. So these were some of the things I was thinking about that day as we drove north on the New York State Thruway with their pop girl-group music blaring from the CD player and the girls singing in the back seat, and I was thinking, too, of the video, repeated on endless news loops that summer, of a young black girl in a bathing suit being slammed to the ground by a white police officer in McKinney, Texas, the two-hundred-pound man pushing that young girl's face into the ground, twisting her arms behind her, holding her down with his knee jammed into her back, and that screaming girl in a bathing suit could have been Essie, she could have been Ebony, and so, of all the many terrible videos unleashed since Errol had been beaten, that one cut hardest, stayed relentless in my mind.

I was thinking, too, about another terrible incident in the news of that summer, what had happened in Charleston on June 17: nine men and women of faith slaughtered at Bible study in Mother Emanuel Church. Nine black Americans murdered by one hate-filled white American. I was thinking about how huge and horrible that news was, and how it seemed to be a call to conscience for the nation—already there were serious efforts underway to remove the Confederate battle flag from the statehouse in South Carolina. And I was thinking that there was probably no one in the country who didn't know about the Charleston slayings, and most would know the name of at least one of the victims, the Reverend Clementa Pinckney; they'd have heard how, at the Reverend Pinckney's funeral only a few weeks before, President Obama sang "Amazing Grace." And I was thinking, *How long will we know it? How long will we mourn? How long will we own our symbols of hatred and say "I repudiate you"?*

And I answered myself: *Not long.*

When the *New York Times* reviewed *Fire in Beulah* in 2001, along with Tim Madigan's nonfiction account of the riot, *Tulsa Burning*, the headline for the review read: "Something Tulsa Forgot." But those first fledging days of research at the Tulsa City-County Library, and my long years of research on lynchings and race riots and Jim Crow that followed, had already taught me: it was not only Tulsa that forgot, and it wasn't just Oklahoma. It was America. The devastation in Tulsa had been front-page news in every newspaper in the country, just as the Charleston slayings were that day as I drove home to the Catskills with the girls. In 1921, the whole nation knew, the whole nation witnessed, and so the great forgetting, the collective amnesia—it belongs to all of us. But of course that's just part of what America forgot.

I didn't talk to the girls about these things then—they were high spirited, ready for summer fun, for the promise of swimming at the town pool the next day, burgers in the yard, the three of us trading off reading Shel Silverstein poems aloud every night before bed: our summertime rituals. I took a picture of the three of us in the yard when we got to our house and texted it to Marlene. This is how I know that the date was July 13. It is from news accounts that I know that that was the same day a young black woman named Sandra Bland was found hanged in a Texas jail cell. She'd been stopped by police three days prior—a routine traffic stop, the media called it, for a routine traffic violation, failure to use her turn signal, and I abhor that word "routine" because I think, yes, routine like Travis being stopped on a routine basis for the same routine excuses, like the routine beating they gave Errol, which had to be routine for how practiced the process afterward seemed—and so this routine stop in Waller County, Texas, led to the arrest of Sandra Bland, and three days later she died in that Texas jail cell. Suicide, they called it. Routine.

We watched the film *Selma* on Netflix one night that week. Ebony and Essence knew all about Martin Luther King, of course—he was part of their history classes, as he had been part of my social studies classes when I was their age. They hadn't known about the violence King and the others faced, hadn't known how brutal the march was. How violent and hate-filled the whole era had been. They were mostly silent on the couch, riveted. They didn't ask many questions. Paul and I tried to give the historical context, how our nation's entire race history gave birth to the brutality they'd seen on the screen. How feeble our attempts were, though.

When I took the girls home at the end of the week, I stayed over at their house in Brooklyn, and Marlene and I talked late into the night about the murders in Charleston, about Sandy Bland and the teenage girl on the ground in her bathing suit in Texas, just as we've always talked about racial events in the news, with grief and frankness and weary outrage. Essence stopped us. She's the younger of the two girls, going on thirteen that summer, and she takes things very much to heart. "I want to ask you something," Essie said. "Where did it come from? The idea that white people are better than black people?"

She didn't ask the question with surprise or wonder or any sense of "oh, that crazy idea." She said it as a statement of fact—she said it as her lived experience. Where did it come from, she wanted to know, this idea that the media, the world, everything that shapes her culture and her education tells her? That white people's lives have more value than black people's.

Then her mother and I talked about slavery. Marlene, the descendant of enslaved people, and I, the descendant of a family that included slaveholders, talked about how that idea—that lie—had been held by white people from the foundation in order to justify "owning" people's bodies, and their labor, into perpetuity. The lie of white supremacy: that is the source of our hidden wound. And it's a lie not just of the past but of the present. A century and a half after Emancipation, we still believe it, and don't know we believe it, because we keep telling ourselves it doesn't exist—at least not in the minds of decent white folks like us. It lives on only in the minds of those white supremacist haters over there, and *they* are not *us*. So we tell ourselves.

In his eulogy for the Reverend Pinckney in Charleston, President Obama spoke of slavery as our country's original sin. And it is that, although many of us in Oklahoma do not forget that there are other sins of equal magnitude—our original sins of genocide and ethnic cleansing against this land's indigenous peoples. In the Southern Baptist church of my childhood, though, there was very little talk of the sin of nations. The wounds of lynchings and Jim Crow, the burnings and bombings of black churches were not spoken about. There was no talk of hate. No mention of what was going on in our country at that time, the beatings and fire-hosings and murders of people who were trying to change things—the ongoing oppression and disenfranchisement of African American people in our nation's long, tortured journey up from slavery. The sins our preachers preached about were personal sins, mostly of the sexual morality variety, and the salvation, the redemption, they promised—that was personal, too.

It wasn't until many years later, when, as a fiction writer, I began to delve into both American history and Scripture, that I came to understand how often Yahweh called His people to repentance. Not just individual sinners, but His people as a people. And I learned that although biblically grace is freely given, redemption has to be earned. John Newton, the slave trader who wrote "Amazing Grace," had his great conversion after a terrible storm at sea. He was facing death, helpless, powerless over what would happen to him, and he turned to God. He humbled himself and prayed and was saved. He was born again. But he kept on captaining slave ships for years after his conversion. That's a part of the story we don't often hear. He didn't turn from his wicked ways until he retired from slaving because of illness. Not because of conscience, or of some great awakening to the moral sin of what he was doing. He just basically got too old and sick to do it. In his later years, of course, he became a powerful voice for abolishing the slave trade. John Newton served as a mentor to some of the greatest abolitionists of his time. But it didn't happen because of his born-again experience. It happened gradually, a spiritual awakening that came about because he tried. He owned what he had done. He turned away from his own past, made an effort to rectify, to atone, in part, by being that voice for change.

To me, that's good news. We can get there by trying. But how? I've been thinking and writing about this a long time. Confession. Repentance. Atonement. Redemption. It's there in *Fire in Beulah*. It's there in *The Mercy Seat*. In my novel *Harpsong*, a character named Harlan Singer lies beside a stream of water, mortally wounded and delirious with pain. He remembers the words of an old man named Profit who had once been his mentor. The old man whispers in Singer's ear a formula for his dying soul's salvation:

> no salvation without redemption, profit says, no redemption
>   without repentance.
> no repentance without confession of sin.
> *what sin?* [the singer's] mind demands.
> no confession without acknowledgment.
> no acknowledgment without pain.

It is going to cost us pain in this country—cost all of us, not just the ones who suffer the consequences of our transgressions right now, but also those of us who think ourselves unsullied, untouched. It requires knowing what we don't want to know, and our part in it. It requires losing our innocence. The collective repentance, the national turning away, has to begin with the individual—and it has to begin in the souls of white folks. How else can it begin? We are the authors of devastation. I grew up with all the privileges and presumptions of whiteness. Acknowledging that, understanding what that means and *owning* it, is my part. I've suffered my own forms of willful ignorance, many ways, many times, and I've also suffered unwilled ignorance—that innocence James Baldwin speaks of. That hidden wound Wendell Berry writes about. My unofficially adopted family—my family of choice—is black. The children I've loved like my own since they were born are black. I've watched them navigate America, with all its racialized challenges, and still I make mistakes. Still I see the world with white eyes—what other eyes am I going to see with? I've been trying for the better part of my adult life to take the blinders of whiteness off. It's so very hard to do. But I keep trying. It's part of why I write what I do, why my novels revolve around narratives of race and bias and discord. It's why my fiction includes voices from cultures outside my own—black and Indian and Mexican—cultures to which I'm bound by ties of love and family and choice. The truth of this place cannot be told without their voices. The effort to touch the souls of white folks like me can't be realized without them.

In the middle of *Fire in Beulah* there's a set piece, seemingly unconnected to the rest of the plot, but in my mind completely integral to it: it's an imagined scene inside a church in Arcadia following the lynching of a young black man from that community. The lynching is historical fact; the church and the pastor Reverend Shew, who preaches the sermon, are imagined. He uses as his text Isaiah 62:

> Thou shalt no more be termed Forsaken; neither shall thy land any more be termed Desolate: but thou shalt be called Hephzibah, and thy land Beulah: for the LORD delighteth in thee, and thy land shall be married.

Beulah, that old-fashioned name we sometimes equate with heaven and sometimes with the Promised Land, means very simply "married." And we are married, here in this great troubled, roiling melting pot. Black and white, indigenous and Asian, Middle Eastern, African, European—the whole world is here in this wounded America.

Thirty-five years after I left Oklahoma, I came home—not just to be here part time, as I'd been doing for decades, but to live here fully, to be a full citizen again, to teach at a university with its own racial wounds. The state I moved back to in 2015 is a different place from the one I left. The lines of separation between black and white and Indian are thinner, but they're still here. We have a growing population of Asian and Hispanic and Middle Eastern Americans now, but in Oklahoma, the dominant culture still dominates. Some here have begun to turn a searchlight on our true history. We tell the story of the riot now, and our history of lynchings, the systematic and systemic disenfranchisement of African American and Native American peoples. We're still uncovering the facts of our past—the facts of the Tulsa Race Riot, for instance, including the fact that the term "riot" is a misnomer, because it began as a race war and turned into a pogrom. I see a new willingness here, in this meat cleaver–shaped place in the viscera of America, to acknowledge the shameful parts of history, the terrible parts that for so many decades we have denied. And that is a good thing. That is a healing thing. But the wounds are still aching.

The author's grandfather Allie Askew (*back row, fourth from the left*) and other asphalt plant workers, September 1924. *(Author's collection.)*

NEAR McALESTER

For years when folks asked me what part of Oklahoma I lived in during the months I stayed here, I'd always answer, "Near McAlester." Our house on a ridge in southeastern Oklahoma is the same distance from Wilburton, and actually closer to Hartshorne, but McAlester is where we'd go to shop, use the library, eat out, get our oil changed. It has the post office I've visited most often, the courthouse I've been inside more than any other. I've set portions of two novels and a short story here. The town is seated deep in my consciousness, its history wedded to my own in ways that are difficult to tease out. The stories blend—fiction I've written, the area's history, parts of my life lived near here, my family's old connections.

My Papaw Allie died here—at McAlester Regional Hospital. In his prime he worked here, at the munitions depot southwest of town. His first cousin Hughie Askew worked as a guard at the prison in the 1930s and was kidnapped by two inmates, shot in the neck, driven in the prison mail truck six miles west of the penitentiary, and let go when the escapees commandeered another car. Cousin Hughie survived. I don't know what happened to the prisoners. My daddy first worked here when he was sixteen, just as World War II was starting. He and Papaw would rise in the predawn hours and drive fifty miles from Red Oak to work at the munitions plant.

At 11:30 most mornings, my rock house a dozen miles east of McAlester will shake suddenly with the sound of distant booms. The windows rattle. Framed photographs slip sideways on the walls. The trembling is like an earthquake, except for the ordered rhythm of the low, thunderous *booms* that precede the vibrations. When my husband and I first heard them, we thought drilling companies were exploding dynamite deep within the earth, fracking for natural gas. It turns out fracking doesn't make that kind of a noise. The booms are, in fact, explosions: old ordnance being destroyed at the same munitions plant where my father and grandfather worked seventy years ago.

Around the time of statehood, I'm told, McAlester's civic leaders had a choice—would they rather have a land-grant college located here or the state penitentiary? They chose the prison because they believed it meant more jobs. Today the prison is one of the area's main employers, along with the munitions plant, which was brought here through political pull and the promise of good available labor—out-of-work coal miners with strong backs, excellent work habits, and hungry families to feed. McAlester has long had a politically powerful history. It was the stomping grounds of Speaker of the House Carl Albert, who in 1963 was a heartbeat away from the presidency, and the birthplace of former governor, lieutenant governor, and favored namesake to countless public buildings and thoroughfares all over Oklahoma, George Nigh. It was also the home of the longest-serving state senator in U.S. history, Gene Stipe.

I like the looks of the town, and the character of its people, a smooth amalgam of southern and western—that signature Oklahoma blend that shows up in their accents, their attitude, their friendliness and style. They're good people, honest, hardworking. In fact, the strong work ethic here is one of the area's calling cards. At a ceremony at the McAlester Army Ammunition Plant honoring a departing commander, he praised the civilian workers, how effective they are at loading and filling warheads, their speed at shipping large amounts of munitions quickly, their efficiency and safety record. When I take my car to my mechanic here, I know the work will be good, the price fair, the assessment honest.

I like the beautiful old Scottish Rite Consistory rising majestic on the town's highest hill: you can see it for miles at night, glowing a lovely amber-rose color. I like the western style of the buildings, the rectangular eminence of the old Aldridge Hotel. I like how close to *now* the town's history remains. McAlester is one of the oldest towns in the state, founded, like so many Indian Territory towns, by an entrepreneurial white man who married an Indian woman. The first opera house west of the Mississippi was located here, but it was torn down to make way for the First Baptist Church parking lot.

Still, much of the original Old West feel remains. You can see it in Old Town on North Main Street, where J. J. McAlester's store still stands with its roofed porch and painted brick sides. The store and its owner make their literary appearance in Charles Portis's novel *True Grit*. McAlester, in fact, has multiple literary connections.

John Berryman, one of America's most influential poets, was born here, spent his childhood here. I like to ponder how the Pulitzer Prize–winning author of *Dream Songs* was shaped by this town. He left at the age of ten, never to return, but maybe McAlester's memory lingered in his sudden moves through rhetorical styles—the elevated language cutting quickly to plain diction, an uncouth tone. Perhaps it lingered in his recollections of Father Boniface, the adored priest under whom he served Mass here six days a week, who appears in Berryman's fiction, his conversation, his poems.

The great African American novelist Ralph Ellison never forgot a journey he took to McAlester as a boy—in a Jim Crow railcar with his mother and younger brother because she'd been promised a job in the town. The job never materialized, and they returned to Oklahoma City, but that ride never left him; it's enshrined in his story "Boy on a Train," where the mother says: "Things are hard for us colored folks, son, and it's just us three alone and we have to stick together. Things is hard, and we have to fight. . . . O Lord, we have to fight!"

In March of 1935, local coal miners and their wives took over the county courthouse here for three days, demanding aid from the government: food and jobs and clothes. I based the climactic scene of my novel *Harpsong* on that siege, which happened, in reality, in the very courthouse where, in 2004, Terry Nichols was tried on state charges for his role in the Oklahoma City bombing. I sat in on those proceedings. Nichols wasn't sentenced to death, as the state's law-and-order predilections would suggest, but to life in prison—which he was already serving at the federal facility at Leavenworth, Kansas, where he was returned to finish out his sentence. I supposed if he's ever paroled, Oklahoma will get him back and send him to die of old age at Big Mac.

If you come to McAlester by way of the Indian Nation Turnpike, you'll pass a statue of a cowboy in prison stripes arched high in the air on the back of a bucking bronco in honor of the annual prison rodeo, for decades the town's biggest tourist draw, although it hasn't been held since 2009—due to cost is the official word, though I suspect there may be more to it than that. If you look north, you'll see the penitentiary itself, a white shimmer on the horizon as you drive into town on a boulevard named for that U.S. congressman who was a heartbeat away from the presidency. You'll pass the red brick courthouse with its U-shaped wings where Terry Nichols was tried, plus a ubiquity of buffaloes: handsome bronzed statues on most every corner honoring the local high school team mascot. If you keep going, you'll bisect George Nigh Expressway.

Don't trouble yourself to look for Gene Stipe Boulevard, though. That street's name was changed back to Electric Avenue after the senator's political demise. Stipe was known to friend and foe alike as the Prince of Darkness, and he was powerful in this state almost beyond reckoning—until he wasn't anymore. He was related to my family by marriage and helped us out in troubled times. Senator Stipe always showed up for funerals and pie suppers, that important southeastern Oklahoma custom where local Masons auction off pies for thousands of dollars to help families in need due to medical bills and lack of health insurance. I have good memories of the Prince of Darkness. He was a marvelous storyteller and could be extremely charming. A powerbroker he may have been, but he always showed up for his people. He showed up for my family.

Every few months, a quiet vigil takes place in McAlester, outside the prison walls, as another man or woman is executed. The anti-death penalty activists, the Quakers and Christians and committed believers, all stand around with their homemade signs and their silence. We only hear about such things when the execution is botched, as it was in the forty-five-minute torturous death of Clayton Lockett in 2014. Otherwise the vigils do not draw much attention.

The prison rodeo drew plenty of attention in its day. Crowds came from all over the country. I remember going as a child and wondering at how the guards and the prisoners seemed to get along so well. I had thought they would be enemies, like the enemies we dropped our bombs on, but they acted like friends. Or at least there, inside the prison walls, in the billowing dust beneath the tall prison lights, amidst the shouts and smells and the announcer's loud metallic voice and the great thundering excitement, they seemed like friends anyway.

Today, all of the conventional bombs our country drops on other countries are made in McAlester, at the same plant where the old bombs and ammunition that haven't been used to destroy enemies are themselves destroyed, to make way for fresh new ones.

In some ways the prison and the munitions plant represent McAlester to me, as McAlester represents Oklahoma, as Oklahoma represents the rest of the nation—each an exquisite distillation of the American character. I love this place, though sometimes not its politics. I love how the past remains alive here, though sometimes I hate our true history. I love the people and the landscapes and the buildings and this state and this little town itself, though sometimes they break my heart.

I used to believe that my dad and granddad made bombs and ammunition to kill enemies during World War II. When I asked Daddy about it, though, he said, no, they worked in construction: they didn't build bombs; they built the buildings where the bombs would be built. My friends and neighbors who work at the munitions plant today probably don't see an Iraqi boy with his arms blown off by one of our bombs, or a slaughtered Afghan wedding party, bride and groom and guests in shreds and bloody pieces, from a U.S. drone strike's mistake.

I don't expect them to. These are good people working good jobs, the best jobs to be had in the area, with decent salaries, benefits, childcare—things people need to take care of their families. I see them, though. The armless boy. The mangled bride. Most mornings around 11:30, when I hear the powerful muted *boom* in the distance, and my house begins to quake.

Just as, when the local news tells me it's time, I see, in my mind's eye, a living, breathing man led in manacles along a blank cinderblock hall into a small room with curtained windows and clinical-looking IV lines and, there in the center beneath bright fluorescent lights, a clean, white-sheeted gurney, surrounded by good people working good jobs.

Measuring the rattlesnake. Front yard of the author's home, Sans Bois Mountains, Thanksgiving Day 2011. *(Author's collection.)*

RHUMBA

We found a baby rattlesnake in the house when we got here one fall—not dead yet but dying, stretched S-like on the large glue board I'd set out to catch the scorpions and daddy longlegs that hold barn dances in our empty house while we're gone. This is my fancy about what the critters do in our absence: dozens of pale tan creatures, barbed tails arced high, sashay their long-legged partners across the living room floor, or lasso and ride the skittery six-inch black centipedes that sometimes scurry along our baseboards flaunting their wicked orange feelers. We find their desiccated corpses under chairs, beneath windows, laid out in the empty laundry basket when we return in the fall. My mind thinks: *What has exhausted them so?* A barn dance. A play party. A Wild West rodeo. More likely it's the poison I spray in the crevices before we close up the house to head north for the summers, but I enjoy the barn-dance fancy.

Our rattlesnake problem isn't fancy, though. It's fact.

"Watch out for the snakes," my husband and I tell each other when we go outside to walk or work. Our rock house sits on a rocky bluff in the Sans Bois Mountains of southeastern Oklahoma. Somewhere north on the ridge behind us is a winter den. If you've seen the rattler scene in *True Grit*, you've got the picture. This land where we live is the same country. The Sans Bois and the Winding Stair are twin ranges: rugged, low, humpbacked mountains slashing east to west above the plains, thick with hickory, oak, southern pine; they hold the same jagged sandstone bluffs and limestone caverns.

When the days shorten, the rattlers come passing through on their way to that hidden crevice, where, until spring, they'll sleep entwined in great complicated knots, moil all over each other, crawl outside to sun themselves on warm days. A group of rattlers gathered together like that is called a rhumba, by the way. A rhumba of rattlesnakes.

On a strangely warm November day in 2011, Paul and I watched a five-foot diamondback crawl out from beneath the ramp to our shed. The snake was beautiful, really, ruddier than most, and as thick around as my forearm, its rattles lifted high as it moved in no particular hurry but with clear purpose, down into a rocky drainage ditch, up again on the far side, continuing across the ridge in obedience to that den's siren song. I come from a people who will not allow any poisonous snake to live. My husband is a city guy from Boston with no family tradition of snake killing. Whether either of us could have brought ourselves to shoot that diamondback is a moot point, however. We didn't have a gun.

My dad had been mentioning this lack ever since we bought the place years ago. He took one look at the rocky ridge behind the house, the huge sandstone slabs that lie tumbled about the property like a giant's toy blocks—a thousand places for a rattler to love—and shook his head. "Y'all might want to think about getting yourselves a gun."

Okay, we'd think about it, we said.

And we did think about it. Talked about it, too. I leaned toward the notion of getting a gun. My husband did not. We have a mixed marriage, you might say. He's East Coast urban culture, where mainly just cops and criminals have guns. I'm rural Oklahoma culture, where pretty much everybody has one. Or several. My dad was always a hunter. When I was a kid growing up, the full six-tiered gun rack on our den wall was as unremarkable to me as the swan-shaped lamp on top of the TV.

That first year we stayed here, I called Daddy and asked him to drive the thirty miles from his house to come kill the blacksnake in our wood box. Blacksnakes aren't poisonous, I knew that, but this one was *huge*, and the wood box is *inside* the house, right next to the woodstove. When I opened it and saw those dusky looped lengths of muscular motionless body curled around stumps of last winter's wood, I dropped that oak lid with a thud and headed for the phone. "We can't be taking a chance on it getting out into the house!" I said by way of explanation to my Yankee husband as I punched in Dad's number.

He brought his Magnum pistol and a five-pronged frog gig and ended up using the gig and a shovel. No sense firing a gun if you don't have to. He chased the snake outside into the yard, then pinned it to the ground with the sharp prongs while he got in a few good whacks with the shovel. "If you're not going to get a gun," Daddy said, "at least get you a good frog gig."

Which we did, not long after. We still have it, fifteen years later, stored in the garden shed where that five-foot rattler crawled out from beneath the ramp. We've never used it to kill a snake.

My sister Ruth and her husband own both gig and guns. They have a rifle, a shotgun, and a handgun Daddy gave them to shoot snakes with. They raise cattle across the pasture from my parents' house on our family's hardscrabble land east of Red Oak, where livestock deaths from coyotes and bobcats are common. Raccoons attack their laying hens at night—a ruthless, bloody slaughter, and only the hens' heads are eaten. Copperheads hide in the weeds beneath the water trough. In the creek beyond the pasture, thick brown water moccasins swim along the top of the water. There are reasons why people here kill poisonous snakes.

That baby rattler we found inside our house was a diamondback, its markings as clearly etched as the top of a matchbox. It could've been the offspring of the rust-colored one Paul and I watched crawl out from beneath our shed ramp the year before. If the glue board hadn't caught it, one of us could have stepped on it in the dark. We always put on slippers when we get up in the night, because of the scorpions, but soft slippers are no protection from snake fangs. Baby rattlers are born dangerous—they'll rear back, whip around, strike repeatedly if they feel threatened. Unlike a grown rattler, a young one has no ability to limit the amount of venom it injects. When I went to discard the glue board, the baby rattler moved. I jumped back about ten feet. The poor thing was nearly flat from starvation; it had probably been caught there for weeks, but the moment I came near, it began slowly, painfully writhing. I grabbed some long cooking tongs to carry the glue board outside, laid it on the stony ground, and ran over it with the car. You can't get sentimental about baby rattlers. Any rattlesnake, really.

I wrote a story once about a fellow who liked to drink in bars in southeastern Oklahoma with a young rattlesnake coiled under his hat: he'd sweep off his hat to reveal the baby rattler, just to shock and impress the ladies. That fiction was based on a true story my dad told about a cowboy snake wrangler from Heavener who did such things, and died from it. When I was researching the story, I learned a few facts. Rattlesnakes can strike two-thirds their own length and get back to coil so fast, the human eye can hardly see it. They have medium-to-poor eyesight, a perfected sense of smell through that constantly flickering tongue, and excellent motion detectors via bones in their jaws that can feel the tiniest mammal footfall. They have acute heat sensors in the pits between eye and nostril—that's what gives them the name "pit viper." When a rattler strikes, its fangs pierce the flesh, instantaneously injecting venom as if through a hypodermic needle. "Venom" is the correct term, of course, not "poison," although locally we still, and probably always will, call them "poisonous" snakes. In humans, a rattlesnake bite is horrifically painful. Symptoms include swelling, hemorrhage, lowered blood pressure, difficulty breathing, increased heart rate, fever, sweating, weakness, giddiness, nausea, vomiting, intense burning pain. Without treatment, death can come within hours.

Most species of rattlesnake—the velvet-tail, the ground rattler, even the eastern diamondback—when disturbed, will try to withdraw. Not the western diamondback: it will stand its ground. It may even advance to get within better striking distance. Western diamondbacks account for the majority of snakebite deaths in the United States. They account for most of the rattlesnakes we see on our mountain. Two weeks after the shed-ramp rattler, we encountered another. This time the whole family was there to witness.

🦌 Thanksgiving Day, 2011—another weirdly warm afternoon in November, the Sans Bois bluffs bathed in southern winds and amber sunshine, and everybody gathered at our house for dinner. In the after-meal lull, with the older folks all sitting around the front room dozing or talking, my four nieces and their little dog set out for a walk to the east pond.

Nineteen-year-old Faith comes in the door after a bit, hunting her camera. "There's a snake coiled in the yard," she says, her voice remarkably calm. Little eight-year-old C.C. marches to the living room, stands in front of my snake-phobic mom, and announces: "There's a big snake in the yard, Grandma. We think it's a rattling one."

Daddy is up from his easy chair and out the door like a shot. I hurry around trying to locate my phone to take pictures while the rest of the family troops out to see it—except for my mother, of course, who wouldn't go out there on a dare.

By the time I reach the porch, the rattler has uncoiled and begun crawling away from the house toward a flat nest of sandstone slabs and boulders beside the pond path. I catch a glimpse of it gliding rapidly through the dead grass, its diamond markings mottled but distinct. Its size is almost beyond belief: even winding S-like that way, the rattler is longer and thicker than any I've ever seen. What's even more unbelievable is the sight of my eighty-six-year-old dad following fast behind it with our frog gig—the one my husband has just helpfully fetched from the garden shed. I can see my dad's back, his bony shoulders hunched as he trails the snake quickly across the yard, and then Daddy's right arm arcs high, the gig handle gripped in his fist like a harpoon as he makes a great downward jab, and everybody gasps, or shouts, "Be careful!" "Watch out!" But those small, sharp metal prongs, designed to pierce a frog's vulnerable back, just bounce off the rattler. No way can they pierce that tough snakeskin. Before Daddy can try again, the rattler disappears into a hollowed-out crevice beneath a giant boulder.

In the pause that follows, we hear the rattles in the dark under the rock, still sizzling. Daddy frowns, bending over to peer inside the crevice. Young Faith, in denim skirt and soft mukluks, circles the rock with her camera. She's a city girl, an aspiring photographer, smart and fearless, at least where animals are concerned. She has no idea of the danger. "Faith!" I call out. "Keep your distance, hon!" She retreats a little ways, camera still clicking. Her mom, my sister Rita, who lives in Tulsa now, far removed from this wild-hearted country, says, "Aw, let's just leave it alone. It'll go on, won't it?"

"Not necessarily," my sister Ruth says, very matter-of-fact. She knows: as stirred up and frightened as it is, that rattler might stay under the rock for hours. Days, even. When would we ever know for sure it was gone? This is rural, mountainous, deep-in-the-bojacks Oklahoma. You're not going to just call up the friendly folks at *Animal Planet* and have them come remove the diamondback from your property. The fact is, we have to kill it.

Trouble is, nobody's got a gun. Paul and I still don't have one. Ruth and Les didn't bring one. Rita and John only get garter snakes in Tulsa. They're not gun people. Our daddy owns three shotguns, a rifle, a muzzle-loader for black powder season, the Magnum pistol he wears in a holster for shooting cottonmouths from his four-wheeler when he's crossing the creek. But for my father, and for most of the men I know around here, a gun is a tool; it serves a specific purpose: to get food for your family, to protect your livestock from coyotes and rattlers. If there's no purpose for the gun, it stays put in the gun rack or behind the basement door. Daddy would never dream of going to the woods without a gun, but he'd also never think to bring one to Thanksgiving dinner.

So. No gun. Kids and dog in the yard. One useless and ineffective frog gig. A riled and lethal and very huge western diamondback holed up under a rock a few dozen yards from the front door. What would *you* do?

This being rural southeastern Oklahoma, what we do is, we call a neighbor. Daddy comes toward me now, the gig laid back against his shoulder. "You reckon Richard and them are down at Dixie's?"

"Sure," I say. "It's Thanksgiving."

"Call down and see if you can borrow a gun."

I quit taking pictures with my phone long enough to use it to call down the mountain to our near neighbor Dixie to ask if we can borrow her son-in-law Richard's gun. "Preferably a shotgun," I tell her, echoing my daddy's instructions in one ear. "Paul will drive down and get it," I say, echoing my husband's words in the other. "Or a twenty-two, a pistol," I say, listening to my dad again. "Just anything. We got a rattler in the yard."

Dixie relays the message to Richard; she comes back on the phone. "No problem," she says, "but y'all don't need to drive down here. Richard says he'll bring his shotgun up there."

Within minutes his tan work truck comes bouncing up the mountain on our pitted gravel road, and I can see a couple of passengers in the cab with him. Well, of course. A rattler in the yard is big news. Richard climbs out of the cab, reaches in and pulls his twelve-gauge from the gun rack, and heads toward us, trailed by a dark-haired young man and an eight-year-old boy, his stepson-in-law and grandson. Because that's how it is here: the necessity and excitement of snake killing gets handed down from man to boy.

Richard steps onto the large sandstone slab in front of the crevice, and my sister and I corral the kids out of the way, positioning ourselves to try to see the snake at the moment of killing, which we can't, of course: the space underneath the boulder is too low, cavernous, shadowy almost to black. Once he has the snake located, Richard doesn't even slow to take aim, but hoists the shotgun to his shoulder and fires in one smooth motion, *ker-poww!* A great blast, followed by a furious, tortured hissing *rattle-rattle-rattle-rattle* as the snake thrashes in the dark, dying, and we all creep forward to see.

The high sizzling buzz, so heart-stopping and terrifying when it comes from a roused rattler ready to strike, seems sad now, feeble, vibrating more and more weakly beneath the ledge. My young nieces utter soft sounds of dismay. The men stand back a smart distance from the black crevice, unperturbed. They know how dangerous a dying rattler can be. When the buzz has slowed to almost nothing, Richard uses the frog gig to drag the body out, jabbing it behind the head and hoisting it up lengthwise for all to see. A murmur of amazement ripples through us. The rattles are silent now, the thrashing stilled to an occasional small tremor, a slow, useless lifting of its tail. Richard lays the snake out on the sandstone slab; we gather in a circle, marveling at its size, how clean the shot is—a neat, bloody wound across the back of the head, keen enough to kill it but not destroy the carcass. The men's voices are calm, their excitement expressed now in dry, understated Okie drawl: "Big snake." "Uh-huh." "Right at six foot, I'd say."

"Can't we just kill it?" Faith keeps saying. "Put it out of its misery? There's a shovel right over there." She's a tenderhearted girl, devoted to all living creatures, especially cats and guinea pigs; she feels the snake's suffering. The men eye the stretched-out body. "Aw, it's dead," Richard says. A snake will keep moving long after its head has been blown off, we all know that, but this one's head is intact, and there's something mighty alive-looking in its eyes. And the fact is, even a dead rattler can strike. We've all heard stories of severed snakes' heads striking and injecting venom because the nerves in the jaws are still alive. So we keep our distance, gradually moving in closer as we become surer the snake is not a threat.

The dying takes a long time. Our conversation stalls on how long it's taking, how many rattles the snake's got and how many have likely broken off over the years. One thing we don't talk about is who will keep that prize snakeskin. Richard shot the rattler. Even if it is on our property, the understanding is that the snake goes to him. I ask to keep the rattles, though, and that, too, seems fitting, or in any case, no one questions what I might want those smelly old rattles for. The men speculate about how long in feet and inches the snake will measure when its muscles finally relax, how thick through the middle it is. "'Bout as big around as a pop can," Richard says. *Thick as my upper arm*, I'm thinking.

When the snake is doorstop dead, I stretch out on the sandstone beside it with my arm laid next to the thickest part to verify the comparison while my husband takes pictures. Faith, too, kneels beside the dead rattler, petting it slowly, the way you might stroke a favored pet. At first I think she wants to know, safely, what a rattlesnake feels like under her hand, but then it occurs to me that what she's really doing is trying to soothe the already dead snake, to say, in some way, she's sorry. Maybe I think this because that's what I feel.

On through the afternoon and into the evening, as Richard loads the dead snake into the back of his pickup to drive it down the mountain and we all troop back inside the house for leftovers and a second helping of pumpkin pie, through the slow letdown after all the excitement, the goodbye hugs, the drawn-out end-of-the-holiday family farewells, I feel a kind of increasingly-sick-to-my-stomach regret. I hate that the snake had to die.

But this is our home, our yard. It's tough enough to step out the door on warm days never knowing if that which can kill you lies in wait on the path to the pond. We couldn't simply walk away from a six-foot diamondback holed up beside that path. Richard told us that his father-in-law, Fred Ezekiel, who built our house, had to clean out a rattlesnake den from the rocky bluff behind the house when he laid the foundation. They're trying to repopulate, maybe, Richard says. Trying to move back in. It's one thing to live on a rattlesnake superhighway, and quite a dangerous other thing to dwell in a house where rattlesnakes gather for their winter rhumba among the very rocks and crevices beside you.

The men never considered anything but that the snake had to be killed. Our mother wouldn't come outside to see it even after it was dead. Later, when we showed her the pictures, she shuddered and dreamed bad snake dreams for a week. The girls, our nieces, a young generation, a city generation, found the snake beautiful. They have never lived on this land. They've been watching PBS nature shows all their lives. Their sympathies were definitely with the snake. And their mom, too, my sister Rita, had to go back into the house before the snake died because she didn't want to see its suffering.

But my sister Ruth, who lives here, stayed right through to the end. She knows what my dad knows. What anyone born and bred to this rough landscape knows: you can't allow that which can kill you to dwell in your living and walking and working space. This is a land without mercy. You might hesitate to kill a rattlesnake, Ruth says, but that rattlesnake would not for an instant hesitate to kill you.

I still have the dried rattles from that diamondback. Richard's stepson-in-law Steven brought them to me the next day after they'd skinned and laid out the snake. He told us it measured five feet ten and a half inches, not missing that six-foot guess by much. Then Paul and I drove into McAlester to buy a gun.

His views on gun ownership had shifted—not out of fear for us, he said, but because of what could have happened to the children: to little eight-year-old C.C., her toddler twin brothers, our young-lady nieces and their small yippy dog. We went to the pawn and ammo shop Richard recommended. The place was packed with men and boys in red hunting caps—it was still deer season—and a few grizzled old characters in full camouflage. We wandered the aisles looking at rifles and shotguns hanging in rows with tags we couldn't read, except for the prices. Hoping for advice, we waited at the counter, listening to the clerks and customers converse in a language we didn't understand—the language of weaponry. After a while my husband and I looked at each other, shrugged our shoulders, and left.

The next Sunday, in Red Oak, I told Daddy we were looking to buy a gun, finally, but we didn't know how to do it. "I'll come with you," he said. "We'll go to Walmart." Then he thought a minute. "No, here, tell you what." He went downstairs to the basement and came back carrying his dad's old twenty-gauge shotgun and handed it to me. So that's part of my inheritance now—my papaw's old rabbit gun. It's stored in the bedroom closet, unloaded, stock down, the shells in a zippered pouch on the top shelf. Paul and I keep saying we're going to take it out and fire it one of these days so we'll know what to do with it when we need it.

The dried rattles I keep on my bookshelf, along with a desiccated scorpion, lying on top of a small Oklahoma-shaped piece of sandstone I found in the road. Not a trophy but a talisman. A reminder. "Watch out for the snakes," my husband and I tell each other on warm days. Inside the house, we watch where we step. We never put a hand or a foot where we can't see what we're getting ready to touch.

A tornado similar to the one that hit Boggy. *(Photo courtesy of the Western History Collections, University of Oklahoma Libraries, Flora 779.)*

View from the site in Boggy Holler where the author's grandfather, Tommy Sides, watched the tornado ride down the mountain and tear through Boggy. Smallwood Mountain is to the right, in the distance. *(Author's collection.)*

THE TORNADO
THAT HIT BOGGY

On the day that President Roosevelt died, a tornado hit Boggy, Oklahoma, and wiped it off the face of the earth. My Uncle Granvil was away working on the railroad when his rented house vanished into splinters, his wife and baby girl sucked skyward. They were found later alive, and survived, but they suffered lasting wounds. Aunt Eula had been thrown against a rock wall; she awoke with broken ribs, a broken leg, an unconscious, bleeding baby, and a newly born terror of storms that would haunt her to the end of her days. Her eleven-month-old daughter, my cousin Wanda Ruth, got "knocked in the head," as the family called it, though who could say by what. She remained in a coma in the hospital, hovering between life and death, for weeks.

But three neighbor children had died because of the storm—the little Prince children, Thelma and James, were killed outright; the Smith boy died a few days later from blood poisoning that set in after a two-by-four went through his leg—and so the Sides family counted themselves lucky.

They were marked by it, though, Granvil and Eula and Wanda Ruth. My mother, who just missed the twister, was marked by it, and her sister Daphne, who got caught in it, and my grandfather, Tommy Sides, who watched it from the porch of his sharecropper house a mile away in Boggy Holler: all the survivors of that little obliterated community were marked. Even I was marked, and I hadn't been born yet. The story of that tornado forged my earliest notions of God, fear, fate, weather, my sense of an unfathomable cosmic orchestration, my understanding of the very nature of story itself.

I never heard it called anything but "the tornado that hit Boggy," though in fact it was one of a spate of twisters that struck the nation's midsection that day, a Thursday, April 12, 1945. Storms raged all through the afternoon and evening, dozens of funnels cutting deadly swaths from Oklahoma to Arkansas to Missouri to Illinois. A hundred and two people died in Oklahoma, twenty-two in Arkansas, seven in Missouri. The number of injured: one thousand and one. Most of downtown Antlers, Oklahoma, was demolished. Sixty-nine people died in that little town alone.

But the community of Boggy—which wasn't even a town, really, just a dozen or so houses, an elementary school, a teacherage, a cemetery, a church—that tiny crossroads farming community five miles north of Red Oak was swept away. It happened not even an hour after Franklin Roosevelt suffered a massive brain hemorrhage in Warm Springs, Georgia, and died. A short while later, halfway around the world, on the island of New Caledonia in the South Pacific, my GI father lay on his cot listening to the radio. "The commander-in-chief is dead," the radio announcer said. He also reported, almost as a postscript, the news of the tornados in America: the many deaths in Oklahoma, the several towns that had been hit, including Boggy, just five miles north of Red Oak, my daddy's hometown.

Well, there's your omniscience. There's your orchestration. I learned it first from my daddy repeating his part of the story. It's hardly wondrous now to learn of events at home from half a world away, but in 1945, to my father, hearing the name Boggy spoken through the crackling airwaves across the vast South Pacific was a wonder beyond wonders. It remained so to me in the 1960s, when I heard this part as a girl—all the more so because I knew that at that time my mother and father, who were two years apart in school, hadn't yet met.

Mostly, though, it's my mother's voice that I hear telling the story. She was there as a witness, although peripherally, and when she tells it, she adds all the significant details: her sister's red coat, the schoolteacher in the outhouse, the milk goat hurled up into a tree. From her I learned that it's sensory details that paint the picture, and also that one needn't be present to bear witness—it's enough to have heard the story told vividly from the living witness's mouth.

My mother was seventeen then, on her way home on the school bus, which was not in fact a bus but an old touring car outfitted to hold the country kids who traveled into Red Oak to the high school because the Boggy school went only to eighth grade. When they passed through Boggy going home, my mother says, the sky looked like it was getting ready to storm: massive dark clouds swirling, that ominous green tint to the air, the strange electric smell. The bus driver had his lights on. It was a little after four o'clock.

By the time the driver let my mother out a mile away in Boggy Holler, turned around, and drove back through the crossroads, Boggy itself, for the most part, was gone. The schoolhouse had vanished. The teacherage next door, where Granvil and Eula lived, had disappeared. The Speights place, the Smiths, the Cutlers, Bernice Davis's house: all blown away. What was left then? Stunned chaos. Weird silence. The milk goat, speared through by a sharpened tree branch, hanging dead in a naked elm tree. Sheets of tin embedded in post oak trunks sliced open like cake. Sticks and boards. Bricks and splinters. The moans and cries of the wounded beginning to sound.

If the principal hadn't let school out early, my mother says, there would have been many more deaths. That sturdy brick building was flattened to the foundation. They didn't measure tornados in those days, but surely, by the completeness of the destruction, the one that hit Boggy was an EF4 or 5. And yet, there were the usual strange twists: the little clapboard church next to the cemetery was untouched, the gravestones left standing. The schoolteacher, Helen Jones, was in the outhouse behind her home. The wooden privy was lifted away from around her, all the hairpins were sucked right out of her hair, but Mrs. Jones suffered not a bruise or a scratch. Her chickens were plucked naked. This is what goes with tornados—capriciousness, their peculiar little quirks. Accident. Orchestration.

The mystery of *if only*. If only one man had made one decision differently, everything could have gone so much differently—and in this case, so much worse.

But Mr. Allen did turn out school, and the children scattered, running toward their homes through the rain and hail and wind. My mother's sister Daphne, called Sissy by the family, ran next door to the teacherage her brother Granvil rented. She was fourteen, a slender, brown-eyed girl, the youngest sister in a family of mostly male siblings. She'd worn her new red coat to school that day—a special Christmas present from her parents, a rarity, a treasure in that poor sharecropping family living out the dregs of the Depression.

As Sissy ran toward Granvil's front porch, an awful stillness settled, the breath seemingly sucked out of her lungs; there was a strange, eerie silence. Then she heard the great freight train roar. Just as she reached for the door handle, the house exploded around her, and Sissy was wrenched backward, tumbling toward the three-foot-high rock wall surrounding the yard. Her red coat was suctioned straight off her back. She felt herself being lifted up, up, the funnel pulling her skyward, until, at the last second, she grabbed hold of the single strand of barbed wire anchored along the top of the wall to keep livestock out.

She held on, the steel barbs cutting her palms, the wind whipping her over the fence one way, back over the fence the other direction, back and forth, back and forth, the funnel roaring, her skin stinging, the splinters and pieces of Boggy sailing through the air around her, and Sissy held on. The funnel passed quickly, it was all over in a twinkling, but to my young aunt clinging to that barbed wire, being whipped from one side of the rock wall to the other, it must have seemed to go on forever.

Up in Boggy Holler, my grandfather, Tommy Sides, stood on the porch looking east into the valley; he'd seen the funnel appear at the peak of Smallwood Mountain off to his right, saw it crest the ridge and roar down toward the crossroads, and Papa Sides was helpless, helpless; he cried out, maybe, raised his hands to God, but the tornado rode down the mountain toward Boggy. Tornados are not supposed to scale mountains—it's an old belief in tornado country that a mountain will offer protection—but I promise you, a tornado *will* dance over a mountain, because the scar stayed there for decades. As a kid, I always looked up to see it whenever we went to decorate the graves at the Boggy cemetery: that treeless swath down the side of the mountain, a jagged, pale, untimbered streak validating all the old stories. The scar is gone now; the timber has grown up and covered it, as the earth will always cover herself. But I remember.

When Papa Sides saw the black funnel churning toward the Boggy school, where his youngest girl was supposed to be in class, he ran to the end of the porch, where his horse was still tethered—he and his son Clarence had just got in from rounding up cows from winter pasture—and Papa grabbed the halter and took off down the hill toward the crossroad. My mother said that people said that the closer Papa got to Boggy, and the more he saw of the devastation—the schoolhouse gone, his son Granvil's house gone, the community scoured to sticks and brickle and dead livestock hanging in trees—he started hollering. The nearer he got, my mother said, the louder he yelled. "What did he yell?" I asked her one time. "I don't know," she said. "They just said he was hollering, yelling a blood-curdling yell." Hollering his grief and fear, is what I think now. His son Warren, my mother's favorite brother, had been killed in the Philippines two months before. His sons Darrel and Harlan were still fighting in Europe. Papa could not bear any more losses. Not one more.

I don't know what happened when he got there, how he found Sissy, who carried Eula and Wanda Ruth to the hospital. I know there was a steady stream of vehicles pouring north from Red Oak, rushing back south toward the highway, traveling fast, carrying the wounded to the hospitals in Poteau and McAlester more than an hour away. I know one of those vehicles belonged to my other grandfather, Allie Askew, my dad's dad, who helped ferry the wounded—that's a part of the story I learned long years later—but how and when and by what means Papa Sides brought his baby girl home, I don't know.

I just know that Sissy slept in the bed with Mama and Papa Sides that night, though she was a big old grown girl, slept shaking, trembling, afraid. They had to give her hair five good washings to get the mud and debris out of her scalp. Mama Sides kept going to the well to draw water to heat on the wood cook stove for more baths. Someone found Sissy's coat under a pile of shattered boards, but the filth pounded into it by the tornado could not be scrubbed out, and they had to throw it away. Sissy kept her terror of storms a long time, my mother says. But not nearly as long as Eula.

After the tornado, Papa Sides moved his family to Red Oak, and so did Granvil. My uncle built a four-room house for Eula and Wanda Ruth across the road from Mama and Papa Sides, raised it himself using his own two hands and boards and nails and cinderblocks saved and salvaged and scrimped for. This was also before I was born. Before Granvil came down with the polio that would cause him to wear a leg brace and walk with a cane for the rest of his life.

I never knew my uncle as a hardy working man who could raise a house with his bare hands. I remember him sitting on the loafers' bench in Red Oak wearing pressed overalls and a straw cowboy hat, his crippled leg in its metal brace stretched out in front of him, his two hands resting on the top of the wooden cane somebody had carved for him. I remember the gravel in his voice, his humor, his teasing, his remarkable memory. I remember him telling me, "Two things you can't build against, Rilla Jo. Fire and wind."

You cannot build against wind, Granvil knew. But you can dig.

The first thing my uncle did, even before he laid the foundation for the house, he went to the southwest corner of where he'd stepped out the ground plan, and he started to dig. By hand, with pick and shovel, in that rocky, rocky ground, Granvil dug a ten-foot-deep storm cellar for Eula. Because she never got over her fear.

When I was a little girl, my sisters and I would spend the night in that house with our aunt and uncle and our cousins Wanda Ruth and Carol Sue. We dreaded it, though, if the weather was stormy, because the moment the sky darkened—before the first crack of thunder, before the first round plops of rain started to fall—Aunt Eula would want to head to the storm cellar. Granvil would talk her out of it if he knew the clouds portended nothing more than a regular rainstorm, but if he wasn't home when the clouds came up, we knew what would happen. Eula would make us come out the back door with her to the grass-covered heap in the yard, like an Indian burial mound, with a gray-painted metal door embedded in one end. She would hoist the heavy door, and down the rickety steps into the dank darkness we'd go—to sit for what seemed like hours on the canvas cots and musty bedding, waiting for the storm to pass. I'll never forget the thick odor of mildew and kerosene, the cool concrete smell. Rows of home-canned green beans in Mason jars lining the shelves. Cobwebs. Daddy longlegs. Brown squishy crickets. How I hated going down there. But my own terrors—of the dank, spidery cellar, the dark corners—never trumped Aunt Eula's own.

Eula has been gone for over two decades, and Uncle Granvil nearly as long. What they knew from surviving the Boggy tornado lives on in me, and what my mother came to know, and my Aunt Sissy. I've tried writing it in fiction, but the story won't bend for me. The details are too fixed, the story at once too confined and too large. Old family stories get distilled to their clearest essence—the red coat, Papa yelling on his horse. Writing fiction, I can intuit how many details are just enough. I can change them. But when the story is true, I can't seem to find which of the complications to leave out.

For instance, I know, through the gleaned omniscience of research, that on that same day, April 12, 1945, around that same hour, but in Germany—halfway around the world in the opposite direction of where my daddy lay on his cot in the South Pacific—a young Jewish boy named Elie Wiesel was settling into his second night of freedom since Buchenwald had been liberated by Patton's Third Army the day before. The boy's guts were cramping, not from starvation now, but from eating the liberators' food. And that part of the story seems important, the distinction between manmade disasters and ones born of nature—those that legal contracts still call Acts of God.

There's this, too: on that same day, an American reporter toured the camp so that he might tell the world about the horrors the liberators found there. "I pray you to believe what I have said about Buchenwald," Edward R. Murrow would say in his broadcast three days later. "I reported what I saw and heard, but only part of it. For most of it, I have no words."

On May 20, 2013, I was walking on my country road in the Catskills, a perfect spring day, the faintest breeze, the cloudless sky a miraculous blue. My husband called my cellphone: "There's a huge tornado getting ready to hit Moore!" I began walking fast, nearly running, tapping numbers into my phone, my closest friends in Oklahoma, out of breath, talking, walking fast. Connie in Edmond: "Yes, we're safe, we're in the basement." Anne in Norman: "Yes, we're watching. We're in a sheltered place across the street from the library." My folks in Red Oak, miles away from the tornado: "Are you watching?" "Yes, we're watching; it's terrible, isn't it?" Hurrying home on my road fifteen hundred miles away to watch in real time, helpless, like Papa Sides from his porch in Boggy Holler, as the mile-wide debris cloud roiled over that misfortunate town.

We all watched together, the same images shared by all of us, because the networks and cable news were all live-streaming KFOR in Oklahoma City. A different kind of omniscience, lived in real time: just as, in real time on a different jeweled Catskill morning, my husband and I watched, as the whole country watched, the second plane hit the tower, watched the World Trade Center crumble in real time, and then again in replay, and again, and again.

Just so, we all—friends and family in Oklahoma, New York, Boston, California—watched in real time as the wide black sweep bore down upon Moore, watched it plow over the town and pull away, growing smaller, smaller and whiter, ribboning out until it vanished in the sky; then we watched the helicopter's first view of the flattened grade school, saying to ourselves, along with the newscasters, *Oh my God, oh my God.*

A few weeks later, I would drive into that devastated area. I had waited until the rescue effort died down to the long, slow recovery; waited till evening, when I thought the workers and gawkers might be gone. It was deep dusk, a quarter moon hanging low in the west. No wind, no sound, except, far in the distance, the hum of a scoop shovel, working by generator lights, dipping its long arm, scooping debris, pivoting, dumping it into a dumpster. But that was blocks away. Well, no, not blocks. There was nothing that looked like a city block. It's true what they say, that photographs cannot do it justice, the force of the devastation, the miles and miles of sticks and splinters, mangled metal, concrete slabs and curved driveways ending in . . . nothing. Desolation. Tiny nails and shards. Here and there, that which is so acutely recognizable: an upside-down washing machine. A bicycle handlebar. A crushed car. But it was the silence that most choked me, and the knowledge that, although there was desolation and destruction as far as I could see, and the lights of Moore were just there, on the outer rim, I really had only barely entered the eastern edge. There were seventeen more miles of it, stretching west. No way even to pass through it. No way to describe it. As Murrow said, trying to bear witness to a different kind of devastation, the manmade kind at Buchenwald: for most of it, I have no words.

This is why we have to tell stories. Where we were when the tornado hit. What the sky looked like. The smell, the sound. The choices we made. Earlier that evening, I'd been at the Moore Public Library. I'd gone there as a writer to talk about my books, but it was a while before we got around to it, because for the first hour, at least, we were telling stories.

The librarian told about hiding with some sixty others in the restrooms in the center of the building as the mile-wide black debris cloud headed straight for them: five and six people to a stall, she said, all crowded on top of one another, and the children placed under the sinks in case the roof caved in. But the roof did not cave in, because the tornado, in its own private unfathomable capriciousness, skirted the library entirely, arced north, and took out half the town.

One woman from the outskirts spoke of lying in bed in the darkness long after the storm had passed—grateful to have a bed, she said; grateful to have a roof above her—listening to gunshots. The police had come by and told her not to worry. It was only the sound of men shooting horses, the ones so severely injured they could not be saved. A mercy. Though it did not feel merciful to her, she said, listening to the *pow*, pause, *pow*, pause, *pow* as she waited all night for her daughter, who'd gone to an elementary school to help rescue children, to make her way back home on foot through the dark, debris-clogged streets.

Another woman had survived three deadly Moore tornados. She told how the 2003 funnel seemed to follow her as she drove frantically home, and how, just as she reached her driveway, the twister lifted the roof off her house, straight up into the air, then dropped it back down exactly square on the walls with a force that busted the windows and crossbeams. She said the recovery efforts for the 2013 tornado were so much more organized than those for the destructive 1999 storm. She said there's little correlation between the amount of devastation people have undergone and their lingering trauma. Some may have lost everything and be out the next day helping their neighbors. Others may have suffered only roof damage, or no damage at all, as they hid in their safe rooms, and yet they emerge terrified, filled with survivor's guilt.

But then I knew that. I learned that from my family's stories about the tornado that hit Boggy. Everyone reacts individually to trauma. Everybody carries scars their own way. I want to tell that to people sometimes when I hear them brag about our state's famed "resilience" in the wake of massive death-dealing storms. Some folks are resilient, yes. Some are not.

A few months after the 2013 Moore tornado, I sat in my Aunt Sissy's living room, listening to her and my mother, both well into their eighties then, talking matter-of-factly about the tornado that hit Boggy sixty-eight years before. No fear in their voices. Hardly any wonder. They spoke of the red coat. The barbed wire fence. The mud beat into Sissy's hair. I listened to their calm voices, their laughter, admiring their resiliency, their cool matter-of-factness.

In my head, though, I still heard the sound of Eula's voice, the drawn-out nasal *oooh* she'd offer when the sky darkened, words she said so often they're burned into my mind like a childhood prayer: "*Oooooh*, I'm scared of storms."

The Green Corn Dance, Trail of Tears
Historic Drama at Tsa-La-Gi, August
1977. *(Photo courtesy of Malcolm Taylor.
Used by permission.)*

Cabin where the author lived on the
Illinois River near Tahlequah, winter
1977. *(Author's collection.)*

Dancer Dewey Dailey at rehearsal,
Trail of Tears Outdoor Drama at
Tsa-La-Gi, summer 1974.
(Author's collection.)

TRAIL

Long after I left Tahlequah, I dreamed about the place. Not just the town, but the earth and waters that surround it. The Tahlequah of my dreams looks nothing like the real landscape. In my dreams the images are primitive, iconic: a dark symbol land. Still, I always know where I am. Usually it's the small cabin above the Illinois River where I once lived. Sometimes it's the steep stone-filled path leading down to the cabin. Except, in reality, there was no such trail. That treacherous footpath above the Illinois belongs to Goats Bluff, miles upriver from where the cabin stood. But the mind will blend. The mind grabs hold of symbols. It tells you what matters. What you long for. What you fear.

There's the Tahlequah of my memory, a place crystallized in the seventh decade of the last century, when I lived there with hippies and rock musicians and Indians and actors and the first gay community I ever knew anything about. I went to school at Northeastern, studied special ed and theater, danced at the Trail of Tears outdoor drama south of town. I picked up trash in the little park below Seminary Hall where Town Branch trickles lively over bright green watercress in springtime, creeps slow and debris-cluttered over quarried stones in high summer. I didn't pick up litter because of any acute environmental consciousness—it was just my work-study job, strolling around campus with a shoulder satchel and a long stick barbed with a nail on the end, stabbing up gum wrappers and red paper Coca-Cola cups and pale golden Coors cans.

There is also the Tahlequah of now, of course, with its bypass roads and corporate fast-food corridor, its tourists and traffic and burgeoning Cherokee tribal complex: a vital place, growing, active—very much changed from the sleepy town I remember. I go there sometimes, to see friends. To search for something. But the Tahlequah of now isn't the place I long for.

When I first moved there, I was told the town's name means Two Will Do in Cherokee. The Cherokees had lost a quarter of their people to suffering, starvation, and disease on the Trail of Tears. When they arrived at the end of that terrible journey, the story goes, three scouts were sent out to discover the best place to set up their new headquarters, their "capital." Two men returned, saying this place here, nestled at the edge of rolling hills near a clear river and running streams, was the best location. The third scout never showed up. Tribal leaders decided that the word of the two who had returned was enough, and they set their capital there, calling it *Ta'ligwu*: Two Will Do. Two Is Enough. I heard this story many times, from many sources, or versions of it. Sometimes the men are called "braves" or "elders." Sometimes they're meeting for council, not going out to search. I believed the story then. I doubt it now. It sounds to me like a white man's story, like the jokey stories I was told as a kid about how Nowata got its name, or Eufaula.

In the Tahlequah of my memory, it is always summer. Say the name, and I see the old Cherokee courthouse on the green lawn of the square, the bustling Shack Cafe and Morgan's Bakery down the street, the busy Safeway store with the tree-shrouded park rising above it, and the street called Choctaw dividing at the cement wall. I see the deep, still waters of Lake Tenkiller miles away, where we used to swim late at night after rehearsals, leaping off the rocks into the black water at Wildcat Point, leaving behind the litter of our own pale golden cans when we piled into our vehicles at dawn. I see the rippling, stone-bedded waters of Baron Fork Creek east of town, remember the blond girl who floated away from our party on an inner tube one summer day stoned on pot and beer and was found later, drowned.

I see the winding green snake of the Illinois River, the dense woods pressing in on all sides, thick with vines and clotted under-growth. I feel the humid air on my skin. My ears buzz with the din of cicadas in the hot afternoons, the relentless *scritch-scritch-scritch* of tree frogs at night. I see an army of black specks marching up my leg from where I've stepped in a nest of newly hatched seed ticks, hear the slaps of paddles on water, the shouts of drunken canoeists coming down the Illinois. "Do you work here?" they ask as I collect their empty beer cans and drop them in a pile on the gravel bar below the cabin. The river is a drinking game to them, a Disney ride, an exotic adventure. "I *live* here," I say.

How long was it before I came to understand that my life was only superimposed on the land? That I was not *of* it, merely *on* it? I don't know. Years, maybe. But I do know when my awakening started—in summer, in the 1970s, when I hung out day and night with the dancers and actors and Cherokee villagers I worked with at Trail.

The full title of the pageant was "The Trail of Tears Historic Drama at Tsa-La-Gi," but most of us just called it Trail, or sometimes Tsalagi (the initial sound pronounced halfway between *dja* and *cha*), which I was told meant "Cherokee" in Cherokee, implying that it was their own name for themselves, though in fact their name in their native language is *Ani-yun-wiya*, "the Real People." Not that anyone explained that to me then.

Tsa-La-Gi was also the name of a place—designated so not by the Cherokee people, but by an organization called the Cherokee National Historical Society, unaffiliated with the tribe, formed in 1962 by a white retired army colonel, Martin Hagerstrand, who was married to a mixed-blood Cherokee woman, the kind and lovely Marion Brown. The site near Park Hill had been the original home of the first school for women west of the Mississippi, the Cherokee National Female Seminary, built in 1851 at the height of Cherokee flourishing after the Trail of Tears, and destroyed by fire in 1887, the same year Congress passed the Dawes Act forcing allotment of tribal lands. Forty-four wooded acres of tall oaks and thick-leaved hickories, the compound featured a museum, a replica of an early-day Cherokee village, and the Tsa-La-Gi Amphitheater, where the Trail of Tears drama was performed. Excavated out of the earth itself, the theater had steeply raked seating so that audiences might look directly down on the action; a lushly wooded mountain, crisscrossed with stone walkways, rising in back of the performance space; and, on either side of the stage, giant turntables on wooden platforms to facilitate scene changes. Not far from the entrance, three enormous columns from the burned seminary stood like haunting *memento mori* amidst the trees.

Some local Cherokee women and their offspring would work all day in the Ancient Village, weaving baskets, demonstrating how to make blowgun darts or play stickball, and then walk across the shaded park to the amphitheater at dusk to perform in the drama as villagers—extras, essentially, who had no speaking parts and were paid less than the actors and dancers, but if they were Indian they did get to go onstage in their own hair and skin. Most of the white female dancers had to sweat under the stage lights in bulky black braided wigs, their skin smeared rust red with a theatrical compound known as Texas Dirt. I was only an understudy dancer, and not a very good one, as I will tell you now and would have told you then, but I tried very hard. My own hair was long and thick and dark enough that I was allowed to go wigless, though I still had to dab a damp sponge in the ruddy powder and smear my face and arms and legs before donning my costume—at least until midsummer, when my tan got dark enough that I could go onstage in my own skin. Halfway between dark and light, that's how I saw myself. The program listed me as part Cherokee because that's what I thought. That's what I'd always been told.

Each evening at eight o'clock, the stage lights came on, the music roared to life, and we all shuffled onto the stage in rags and tattered blankets, reenacting the forced march of the Cherokees from their homelands to this territory in the West. The full cast trudged slowly through ominously lit space to the accompaniment of dirge-like music while the white actors who played Cherokee leaders began to orate. We'd stumble and collapse, some few of us dying dramatically and being carried off—a bit of staged business we'd negotiate ahead of time, because it was our only chance to grab the audience's attention. Offstage, we'd sit on the concrete ramps leading to the turntables, our skirts hiked to our thighs or our shirts open, the scratchy blankets thrown aside as we sweated in the sultry evening heat, smoking cigarettes, flirting, fooling around. I didn't then think it an insult to make an entertainment of that brutal act of ethnic cleansing, that American-made death march known as the Trail of Tears. It was my understanding that the tribe approved of the drama, and none of the villagers seemed bothered by our lack of reverence. And anyway, the history in the play was true. More or less.

The script in those years, and for most of the amphitheater's history, was an epic melodrama by a white professor named Kermit Hunter, who had also penned the script for a twin pageant in North Carolina about the Cherokees in the years before Removal. It was a white man's version of Indian history, told simplistically, if sympathetically, with spectacular special effects—dance! music! costumes! flash pots in the Civil War scenes!—but none of that bothered me. It was, after all, a pageant: by definition a colorful public spectacle demonstrating the history of a place. I did object to the fact that there was only one significant female character, a sappy love interest named Sarah who spends most of the play acting like as big a ninny as any white female character in an old western. I also didn't much care for how the Green Corn Dance had us all stooping over and whooping like bad imitations of Hiawatha and Pocahontas to a pounding Russian composition by Shostakovich. Overall, though, I loved working at Trail.

My nights were filled with excitement and performances and partying and learning people's ways I'd never known before. The choreographer was a wonderfully flamboyant Jewish man from New York City named Marvin who taught me words like *schmatta* and *mensch*. I felt ushered into a secret world with my gay friends, a kind of parallel hidden society that had been around from time immemorial, though I'd never known it. The dancers, both gay and straight, accepted me. They were kind to me, actually. Sometimes I wondered at how these performers who'd been training all their lives could be so tolerant of a clumsy girl who couldn't tell step-ball-change from chassé, or execute either very well. But they plopped their dance bags next to mine on the gym floor at rehearsals, showed me how to stretch my muscles without pulling a hamstring, how to wrap my ankles, avoid shin splints. I felt at once inside and outside, a part of and apart from.

I can't say at what point I began to be uncomfortable with how the tragedy was told, the message the audiences left with. In the play, after much fighting and killing between Cherokee factions and a great deal of flashy spectacle, the story ends with the Cherokee people and the white citizens of Oklahoma uniting joyfully on the first day of statehood in 1907. The Cherokees are relieved and happy; they dress up in straw boaters and bustles, and dance a celebratory ragtime dance. The music swells, and Sarah's voice, cracked with age, weighted with wisdom, comes over the loudspeakers to tell the audience, in an astonishing mixing of metaphors, that the Cherokee people did not die in 1907 but were reborn, like the ancient phoenix: "The red man is like a crimson thread running through the texture of this new state . . . like red flowers growing on the green bosom of Oklahoma." And the largely white audiences shake themselves loose from the dream, climb the steep stairs to return to their tour buses and cars believing this is all to the good: no more sorrow, no more deadly divisions between the Cherokees, no more white folks taking away Indian homelands. A blessedly unified peaceable world on the shining green breast of Oklahoma.

Except, I grew up here. I knew it wasn't so.

I couldn't then have named for you the kinds of troubles that lay ahead for Indian people in Oklahoma after 1907—the Osage Reign of Terror in the 1920s, for instance, when scores of Osages would be murdered for their oil headrights; or the federal relocation policies of the 1950s and '60s, when Indian families would be relocated from their allotted lands to distant urban areas, as Wilma Mankiller's family was moved to San Francisco in 1956; or the chillingly named "termination" policies that would continue to steal Indian children by systematically adopting them away from their tribes into "civilized" white homes; not to mention the pervasive poverty, the lack of self-determination, the relentless leaching away of Indian lands. But I knew intuitively, and by witness, the power of racial bias in this state. I'd seen it growing up in Bartlesville, living in Shawnee, Tulsa, Tahlequah—more subtle for Indian people than for black people, true, but it was surely there, a wordless color hierarchy within the dominant culture that said the darker your natural skin color, the lower your status.

It may be hard for some contemporary readers to recognize the racist underpinnings of a state that today proudly proclaims itself to be "Native America" and uses a sanitized version of Indian history to draw tourists, a place where half the white population claims the ubiquitous "Cherokee" great-grandmother. I don't know why *Cherokee* became the proprietary eponym for *Indian*, but it happened long before my time, along with the obligatory "high cheekbones" proof of such ancestry, as my Papaw Allie always pointed to on his own face. His supposedly part-Cherokee mother was born in Texas and migrated to Indian Territory with her family as a young girl—and, yes, from her pictures I believe she could have been part Indian; and, yes, there were Cherokees in Texas in the mid-1800s, a few, but there were also Comanches and Wichitas and Caddos and Tonkawas and other tribes you don't hear white people claiming to be "part" of. Maybe it's because the word *Cherokee* sounds so nice in English—it's easy to pronounce, has a satisfying throat click in the middle, and white history has proclaimed the Cherokees to be a "civilized" nation, so somehow that led to the adoption, even in my grandfather's still very prejudiced era, of Cherokee as the only acceptable tribe to be from—if one were going to claim to be Indian at all.

The 1970s were a transitional period between the overt racism of my great-grandparents' day, when some families may have denied their Indian blood because they thought it not good or smart to be Indian, to the tremendous surge of Native American wannabes today. Even in the '70s it was acceptable, though not yet chichi, to be of Indian descent. But the bias against full-bloods remained. I could hear it in the racist "drunk Indian" jokes told by white friends, see it in the faces of certain dark-skinned kids who were bullied or ostracized at school. The progression from covert prejudice to it's-cool-to-be-Indian accelerated rapidly toward the end of the century, a cultural shift that was hard to miss. I've often remarked that when I left Oklahoma in 1980, nobody was Indian. When I came back in the 1990s, everybody was.

But in Tahlequah, and especially those summers at Trail, it seemed to me that traditional Cherokees and those of us from the dominant culture lived side by side, our worlds superimposed one on the other, as my life on the river was superimposed on the landscape, but our realities did not touch. Somehow either they or we were a hologram. Many of the performers were of Indian descent, proud of their heritage, but white in their way of being. Others looked as white as I did, or more so—pale skin, auburn hair—and yet had more kinship to Indian ways than others with greater blood quantum. There was an unfathomable difference, which I felt but could not name. The layers were beyond my ken: there was a social layer, how we all behaved with one another; a layer of ceremony and tradition, which I heard about but was not privy to; layers of politics, sentiment, romanticism, culture; a hidden spirit layer that was palpable to me but outside my grasp. I felt it most acutely in the natural world around Tahlequah, the hills cradling the town, the rivers and streams that lace through there, the thick woods closing in on all sides. I sensed it in the shaded grounds of the complex itself, with its ghostly post oak trees, its charred brick columns from the old Female Seminary standing sentinel as the tourists filed back to their buses in the dark.

My first summer at Trail there were two star dancers, Eddie Burgess and Dewey Dailey. Both were Indian, both stunningly talented—gifted beyond the level of ability one might expect at an outdoor drama. Their dancing dominated each night's performance. They were point and counterpoint, darkness and light: Eddie, compact, muscular, was the Death Dancer who followed the Cherokees through all their dark days on the Trail, shaking his rattles, taunting them, leaping and tumbling about the stage in scenes of death and destruction. Dewey, long and lithe and graceful as a Balanchine, was the Phoenix who rises from the ashes at the end of the play. These days I can't imagine not knowing the tribes of any of my Indian friends, but in those days I didn't think about it. I never asked what tribe they were, whether or not either of them was Cherokee.

Eddie and I had grown up together in the same Oak Park neighborhood in Bartlesville; his house was just a few blocks from mine, his younger brother in the same class as my sister. I hadn't known him well then because he was a couple of years behind me in school,

but I did know he was a fabulous gymnast. It was Eddie's gym mastery, incorporated into the dance, that made his performa so breathtaking. He had an almost terrifying skill. He rolled a tumbled about the stage in a kind of controlled frenzy that see to me at once balletic and thrillingly wild. Eddie partied as ha any of us (in that summer stock milieu, drinking and carousin, just what we did), but he was also the hardest-working perforn I'd ever seen in my life. The first to arrive at the theater, he'd be warmed up and ready to go, having practiced some uncountabl amount of time by dusky evening, when we all came sauntering chattering in. His girlfriend, Cindy, is one of the dancers I especi remember as being kind to me that summer, and so was Eddie, i fact, though he was so much the star and had the authority of da captain besides, with that incredibly ferocious work ethic, that I recall admiring him more from afar than as someone from inside circle.

Dewey was simply beautiful: sculpted face, arched brows, lush lips. The first time I saw the musician Prince, I thought, God, he looks like Dewey Dailey. In fact, though, to me, Dewey was even more beautiful than that. His performances as the Phoenix were exquisite: feathered, weightless, lighter than air. He seemed to soai beyond the reach of gravity, the symbolic creature who does battle with Death near the end of the travails, is vanquished, burned in the fire, but rises again from the ashes, transfigured to a small Indian boy on a shield, lifted above the heads of the dancers in a triumphant drum-pounding, brass-thrilling, heart-racing theatrica climax at play's end.

Night after night, we dancers ran in circles around the leaping, pirouetting, half-flying Phoenix, flapping our sheer red and orange and yellow flags—the *schmattas* of Marvin's designation—like flames of fire around the dying bird. Night after night, Dewey died in the flames, and night after night, he was reborn as one of the little Cherokee villager boys raised up on a shield. Night after night, Sarah's aged voice came over the loudspeaker to declare that the Cherokees had always believed that the "Great Spirit" had destined them to do "one great thing," and to suggest it was perhaps this, the

creation of this new state of Oklahoma, that fulfilled their destiny. And night after night, in bustle and gingham skirt, I kicked and strutted that two-step ragtime "1907" with a silent, inarticulate rebellion in my chest, an inchoate sense of wrongness: surely the Cherokee people did not see it this way.

How could they? Statehood meant further destruction of the Nation, more land theft, the complete usurpation of self-determination. It meant this land they had suffered so terribly to reach was no longer Indian Territory: in a brutal transmogrification of two Choctaw words meaning "red people," the place was now White Man's Land.

I don't mean to say I was outraged back then, or that I understood yet how my own family's migration into I.T. in the late 1800s was part of the relentless story of theft and displacement, or that I was attuned to how thoroughly white-biased and appropriated the script at Trail of Tears was. I mean only that I'd started seeing things in a new way. I mean that, deep inside me, an awakening had begun—an awakening that was as much artistic as it was social or political, because I loved what Eddie and Dewey did on the stage every night. The acting in the play was heavy-handed, I thought, oratorical, overwrought. The choreography was a New Yorker's stereotyped vision of how to evoke Indian dances, even though, yes, we had shell shakers in the Green Corn Dance—Cherokee women with heavy pebble-filled turtle shells strapped to their calves—and there was a dance called the Ribbon Dance that had the men and women in beribboned "tear" shirts and dresses, though the movements looked rather like a European maypole dance. But the sheer artistry of those two dancers, night after night, took my breath away. Death Dancer and Phoenix. Darkness and Light. Destruction and Survival. Their unending duel, vanquishment, triumph epitomized the layers of spirit and story I could perceive but not name.

The last summer I danced at Trail was 1977. That was the summer Elvis died, and New York City went dark in a blackout that wrapped the city in violence and fear. The summer Florida voters heeded Anita Bryant's anti-gay crusade and repealed their gay rights ordinance. The summer three little girls were brutally murdered at

a Girl Scout camp near Locust Grove, and a Cherokee man named Gene Leroy Hart hid out in the hills north of Tahlequah, evading capture for that horrific crime, which many locals said he did not commit. I heard talk. The Little People hid him, they said. No, others countered: it was the old Cherokee full-bloods living deep in the hills who kept the fugitive from being found. Some said Hart himself was *stigini*, a shapeshifter, a night-walker-about.

Hart's disappearance seemed, that summer, another part of the ineffable mystery, another layer of what I could not understand. There were haunting, persistent rumors. He would never be found, some said. He was a modern-day Ned Christie, a Cherokee man unfairly declared an outlaw by white man's law but not by his own. Others hated and feared him, had convicted him already in their minds because of the news stories. Details of the manhunt covered the news every day, along with veiled rehashings of the unspeakable crimes against three innocent little girls, nine and ten years old, a tragic, horrific outrage, an unbearable heartbreak for their families that I could not comprehend. I could hardly bear to think of it. How could someone, *anyone*, do such a thing?

We know the ending now, or part of it, anyway, what eventually was told in the news: how Hart would elude the searchers well after summer's end, through the winter and into the following spring, when he would be captured and brought to trial. How he would be acquitted of the Girl Scout murders for lack of evidence but sent to the McAlester State Penitentiary anyway to serve out time on a prior conviction. And how, three months after that, he would fall dead of a heart attack while running laps in the prison yard, which some said was inmate justice, covered up, and others said, no, it was Cherokee justice, because Hart really did do those terrible murders, and Cherokee medicine had taken care of him in that way.

I don't know the truth now, any more than I knew it then, that last summer in Tahlequah, when Hart was a fugitive hiding in a landscape of clotted undergrowth and clear running streams—like the area where I lived with my boyfriend in an isolated cabin on the banks of the Illinois. I thought of him out there sometimes. If I happened to awaken on a moonless night, say, to lie in darkness as thick as a wall, listening to the night sounds all around me: the tree frogs' insistent chorus, rhythmic and relentless as torture; the scrabbling of tiny mouse feet in the pine rafters overhead; the low, repetitive hoot of an owl in the trees across the river. I don't remember being afraid. Only watchful. Only listening. I began to understand in a feeling way, a wordless gut- and dream-level way, that I was no more a part of the landscape than the weekend float-trippers. I was only passing through, my life merely superimposed here. I was the hologram. The night sounds could have been anything, I told myself: animal creatures, human fugitive, or something more intangible and dangerous—a shapeshifter, perhaps. But if so, it didn't have anything to do with me. I wouldn't be vulnerable. I was too white.

The next summer I worked at the Oklahoma Summer Arts Institute at Quartz Mountain, where I met Cheyenne poet Lance Henson, the first writer who made me believe I could be one, too. My job included serving as liaison to the drama teacher. I still had theater stars in my eyes, and when I returned to Tahlequah, I immediately packed my bags and moved to Tulsa, intent on working a few months and saving enough money to get to New York. I ended up staying in Tulsa for two years, but I did eventually make it to Manhattan, and studied acting, and ultimately turned to writing. But I kept coming home.

In 1989 my first published story, "The Gift," about a mixed-blood Cherokee boy who descends a steep, treacherous path to a cabin above a river, appeared in *Nimrod*'s spring "Oklahoma Indian Markings" issue. Those same pages are where I first read a Joy Harjo poem. It's where I met the work of Linda Hogan, Joe Dale Tate Nevaquaya, Louis Littlecoon Oliver; where I first saw the gripping photographs of Richard Ray Whitman, the drawings of Shan Goshorn. Later that year, in December, I attended the Modern Language Association conference in Washington, D.C., because the brochure I'd received in my mailbox at Brooklyn College included a listing for a gathering of Indian writers: "Readings by Emerging American Indian Poets." That listing was the only reason I went.

I sat in the back of the conference room, shy and self-conscious, acutely aware of my separation. My aloneness. In the front rows, the writers all sat together. I could see the backs of their heads as they leaned toward each other, their long hair fanned out on their shoulders as they laughed together. They were familiar to me in a way that no one else in that room was, none of the other white teachers, academics, students. I couldn't hear what they were laughing about, but I knew the kind of laughter it was, could hear it in my mind, that dry, ironical *aaaayyy* Indian humor. The feeling I had as I watched them was like going home after a very long time away. Like being almost there.

Yuchi poet Joe Dale Tate Nevaquaya was one of the writers; his brother Richard Ray Whitman also read, and Elizabeth Woody, Carter Revard, many wonderful writers. When Joe read his poems, though, I had an experience, heart-catching, indefinable, that burned the poem into me, not with intellect but in silence, in fiery recognition. I can't explain it exactly, but it happened that night and every time I've heard him read his poems since. Afterward I lingered at the edge of the crowd angling forward to talk to the writers. I wasn't leaving, but I also didn't know anyone to talk to, or what to say if I did. Joe Dale was standing off to one side near the front, leaning against a wall, quiet and watchful; his separation from the others made him seem as alone and shy as I felt. I went up and told him how much I'd enjoyed his reading. We started talking, I don't recall about what—it wouldn't have been poetry, because I'm inarticulate on that score; very likely it was about where we're from, the Oklahoma we grew up in. Later, as the writers were all making plans to go out to a restaurant, his brother Richard Ray (I didn't know yet they were brothers) said to me, "You coming?" I said, "Um . . . yeah!"

For a few hours, a bunch of us sat at pushed-together tables in a D.C. restaurant, talking as hard and fast as we could talk, laughing and joking, and the feeling I had was one of familiarity and discovery, and also of coming home. When the place closed, we spilled out onto the sidewalk, where snow was beginning to fall. We all milled about in the snow-sifted light, still laughing, still joking, exchanging phone numbers and trying to recall directions to our various hotels. I had my car because I'd driven down from New York, but they'd all flown in from Oklahoma, St. Louis, Washington State, so it took a while for everyone to sort themselves into various cabs for the trips to their hotels. Moments later I stopped at a red light and glanced over at the vehicle idling next to me, a checkered taxi, where I saw Joe Dale and Richard and some others in the back seat waving at me; we all waved and laughed, rolled down our windows to holler at one another, till the light changed, and they went their way, and I went mine.

Long months later, on a summer night in his mother's backyard in Oklahoma City, during one of our long, late-into-the-night word-firing conversations that made my heart and the top of my head feel like they could explode, Joe Dale and I talked about that evening, the final hours of the year, the very decade, and he said, "The universe shifted that night." I said, "Oh, yes."

Because, for me, it was true. Looking back, there are only a few things I know for sure about my journey to becoming a writer, and one is that the first most powerful influence on that journey was my husband, and the second most powerful was Joe Dale Tate Nevaquaya. In concentric radiating circles, the influences ripple out from there. I wouldn't be the writer I am or write what I do without those friendships that forged and shaped me, the ones that began that snowy night in Washington, D.C. The first Oklahoma writers I knew were Indian writers. They were the first to make me see, through their words, friendship, books, poems, passionate discussions deep into the night, what this place is, what it has been, what we are all doing here, or trying to do. To this day, they're the community I feel most . . . well, not a part of. Not apart from. They're where my heart is. Their imprint on me is unchangeable. They were the first pure artists I'd known, the first "makers," whose very way of seeing is art, and back before them, there were Eddie Burgess and Dewey Dailey and their exquisite artistry at the Trail of Tears Historic Drama at Tsa-La-Gi.

Eddie left Oklahoma, as I did, to pursue an artistic career. We met for drinks one night in New York in 1981. We talked about Trail, the people we'd known, how far it felt like we'd come. He was dancing with a New York Company then, Jennifer Muller/The Works. Later he would travel the world as a dancer and teacher and eventually become the respected and beloved chairman of the Dance Department at the University of Wisconsin–Milwaukee's Peck School of the Arts. A photograph of him at the barre with other dancers shows a warm, affable smile, a sleek bald head, a fringe of gray hair, and, still, that compact, ferocious dancer's body, even in middle age. It's strange to see him that way, so different from the dark longhaired young dancer he was when I last saw him, and yet the same. The photo is on his memorial page, along with testimonials from other dancers whose lives Eddie touched, because he's gone now. He died too young, in his sleep, at the age of fifty-eight. His bio on the website doesn't mention that he was full-blood Cherokee.

I don't have a middle-aged picture of Dewey Dailey to contrast with my memories. Dewey was Otoe-Missouria/Kaw and Muncie. He, too, died young, even younger than Eddie, in Dallas, from complications related to HIV. In my mind, though, I can't see him any way except as the soaring, unfettered, red-and-white-winged Phoenix. Like Tahlequah itself, Dewey is crystallized in my mind at the height of his young beauty.

When I return now, I drive by the old haunts looking for what has changed and what hasn't. Some places have vanished, like Sixkiller's Barbecue and the tiny frame rental house on Allen Road where I once lived. Some have been transformed, like the old Quik-Trip on Goingsnake, which is now an administrative building for Northeastern. Some remain the same. In the park below Seminary Hall, Town Branch still rushes or trickles over the stones, depending on the season; the watercress is still a bright springtime green; campus litter still catches in sluggish rotations in the slow eddies in summer. South of town, the fast-food joints are strung now like bright corporate Legos from the bypass nearly all the way to the Cherokee Nation tribal complex, an area that was lush countryside back when I lived there.

Sometimes I turn east off that corporate corridor toward Park Hill, winding my way along the two-lane blacktop to the Cherokee Historical Center. That's what they call Tsa-La-Gi now, and it very much lives up to its name: a beautiful native stone museum with a permanent, historically accurate exhibit about the Trail of Tears, a newly built village where visitors can see the same kinds of flint-knapping, basket-weaving, and stickball demonstrations tourists saw in the Ancient Village, but with a difference—there is in the atmosphere, it seems to me, a kind of pride and autonomy, an authenticity of ownership I didn't feel at the outdoor drama back when I danced at Trail. The three giant columns from the Cherokee National Female Seminary stand where they've always stood, in a place of honor in front of the museum.

If you walk around back, through the tree-shrouded parking lots and beyond, you can just see the mottled gray roof of the amphitheater rising barely above the earth. Bypass the yellow caution tape sealing the area off for safety, angle your way around to the west, where the tape has deteriorated and begun to sag, and you can enter the amphitheater at the end of the dim covered hallway where the audiences once went in. The wooden slats at the bottom of the housing are ragged, eaten away, black with damp and mold. Everywhere there is the odor of mildew, rotting wood. Here the audiences would wind their way around the perimeter to their numbered rows, line up during intermission for popcorn and hotdogs and the colorful souvenir programs that told all about the Trail of Tears, stand in urgent lines snaking from the restroom doorways into the crowded hall. If you move through the shadowed space to the open archway, you can look down onto the stage, where small trees and sumac bushes are growing up through the asphalt. The giant overhead fans are broken, hanging loose from their moorings. The loudspeakers, where Sarah's voice came on to tell audiences about the Cherokees' destiny, have been torn out, wires dangling from the sound booth. The scoop-backed chairs, what remains of them, are faded, mildew-stained, tipped over. And the little mountain behind the stage, where the Death Dancer once shook his rattles in the searing lights and leapt and tumbled in an orchestration of death-defying movement and sound, is as overgrown as a jungle, chaotic, forbidding. All is rot and deterioration, the slow leaching away, through years of sun and cold, drought and rain, of what had been built here. In the distance you can hear the shouts of the stickball players inside the village—Cherokee players, men and boys, their cries of triumph, their joking laughter, just as it should be. As it should always have been.

I never go back to the river to see if the cabin is still there. I think I know it isn't—the place was decrepit, little more than a tarpaper shack, even when I lived there decades ago. It lives on in my memory, though, that cramped one-room cabin and the treacherous path leading down to it—a trail that, in reality, doesn't exist. Except in my dreams. Except in my stories. The steep rock-strewn path where a young mixed-blood boy is carried down to the cabin under his father's arm in "The Gift." The home, in my novel *Harpsong*, of Calm Bledsoe, a mixed-blood Cherokee trapper who is murdered by white thieves. These places are seated deep within me; they're not the landscape of my heart but a dreamscape seared in my subconscious, my memory, waiting to be dreamed awake.

Connie Squires and the author, Medicine Park, Oklahoma, August 7, 2001.
(Author's collection.)

Photo display at James Foley memorial, Rochester, New Hampshire, on what would
have been Jim's forty-first birthday, October 18, 2014. *(Author's collection.)*

GERONIMO

We headed south from McAlester to the Texas border in early morning. The day was blazing hot, humid, no wind. Typical August. There was no sense of foreboding. I was driving, my husband navigating, a division of labor we've been using since our honeymoon. Somewhere below the Red River we turned west, and the sunburned plains opened before us. We passed a Justin Boots outlet just off the highway. Paul said, "Whoa, turn back." I did, and we went in, and he bought me a pair of brown cowboy boots for my anniversary present. This is how I remember what the date was. August 6, 2001. Hiroshima Day. Our eighteenth anniversary. The day George W. Bush received an intelligence briefing that said: "Bin Laden Determined to Strike in US."

My family calls me the family historian. I'm always saying, "Oh, *that* happened *then*, I remember, because that was when . . ." Events are strung together in my memory like beads on an endless spiral, which is Time, which is an elliptical ever-turning wheel where the seasons mark their locations in color. August is a wan season, fading ocher and beige. This was the same August road trip when my friend Connie tried to take me to see Geronimo's grave. We weren't allowed. The base at Fort Sill was closed to visitors—a circumstance that puzzled Connie, shook me. That memory is our small piece of the national narrative, or one of them. It's the thing that makes me know there is more to know.

But first:

We met up with Connie and Steve in Archer City, Texas. They were relatively new friends to us then, Constance Squires and Steve Garrison. We had all met the year before, when I served as artist-in-residence at the University of Central Oklahoma in Edmond, where Steve was chair of the English Department and Connie was working on her first novel set in Oklahoma. They had roots and histories in places like mine, book and poetry passions akin to Paul's, and this was our first road trip together—a pilgrimage to Larry McMurtry's famous book town on the West Texas plains. Connie and Steve had trekked some three hours south from Edmond; Paul and I drove nearly five from McAlester in order to meet for lunch at the Archer City Dairy Queen. They had both read McMurtry's *Walter Benjamin at the Dairy Queen*, Paul and I had not, but we all raised a metaphorical toast to philosophy and storytelling and youths spent habituating soft-serve drive-ins before we fanned out to scour the bookstores.

In those days there were still four large buildings called Booked Up around Archer City's town square, each designated by a number: 1, 2, 3, and 4. Book palaces, really, shelved floor to ceiling with used volumes organized to a bibliophile's exacting demands. Through the long afternoon we browsed and perused, gathered armloads of books, wandered from store to store, losing one another in the stacks, coming back together again. We were each working with a subtext, though I don't think we talked about it that way. Paul was seeking a rare volume of poems by his friend Grandin Conover, who'd committed suicide in 1969. Connie was on the hunt for Iris Murdoch. Steve grew up in West Texas and was a fan of McMurtry's on a level beyond fandom: the man had been writing Steve's own mythic family territory all his life. As for me, I had an overdue debt to pay.

In the late afternoon, as the heat and humidity grew unbearable and we were passing from one shade awning to another, we spied the great man himself, in suspenders and shirt sleeves, trundling a load of books on a dolly across the sweltering sun-bright street. Though I had half hoped to see him, I hadn't really expected that I would. Certainly I hadn't thought I would find him this way, on a nondescript workday with the West Texas sun bearing down as he wheeled a heavy load of cardboard boxes across the street like a UPS delivery man. When he reached the far side, he reversed the dolly and dragged the load backward up over the curb. Then he disappeared into Booked Up No. 1.

Steve said, "Here's your chance!"

"Really?" I said. "You don't think it's too, I don't know ... *invasive*?"

"I think he'll appreciate it. When are you ever going to have a chance like this again?"

I looked at Paul. He shrugged. I looked at Connie, who offered a quick little *why not?* grin. Back to Steve, who nodded his encouragement. "Okay," I said, and we all trooped across the street to the main store, where the rare antiquarian books were kept, and where you were to carry your stash of books you'd gleaned from Booked Up Numbers 2, 3, and 4 to pay for them. For all the manpower spent organizing and cataloguing the volumes, little was spent on operating cash registers, it seemed. The whole enterprise was based on the honor system, as if it stood to reason that anyone willing to drive several hours across barren plains to reach a book town would necessarily be a person honest enough to pay for them. Inside the store, the great man was nowhere to be seen.

We set our stacks of books on the cashier's counter and continued shopping, edging along the aisles, heads tilted back to read the titles. I kept an ambivalent eye out. I wanted to see him, and I didn't. When my first book, *Strange Business*, a collection of short stories about life in a fading southwestern small town, came out in 1992, Larry McMurtry gave it a lovely blurb: "Very original and very moving. This is a most promising talent." I never thanked him. I never sent a handwritten note, as would have been most proper, nor even extended a word of thanks through my young editor, who was the one who'd sent him the galleys. The fact is, I'd been so ignorant and naïve and overwhelmed at getting published in the first place, and so in awe of a writer of Mr. McMurtry's stature—he was like the sun to me, like gravity: a natural force—that it never occurred to me that I should.

And so now, nearly ten years later, in McMurtry's own fading *Last Picture Show* hometown, with my debtor's sense of guilt gnawing at me and the recollection of Steve's voice at lunch saying, "Do you know how rare that is? What a compliment? He just doesn't *give* blurbs!" and despite the printed signs tacked up in all the stores delineating a few simple rules of etiquette for shoppers, the main one being DO NOT SPEAK TO THE OWNER, I could see that this really was my chance to make amends. When Steve eased by and told me he'd spied McMurtry sorting books in the warehouse-like area attached to the back of the store, I made my way in that direction. We all four did, and paused, and grazed a few aisles away, trying to look engrossed in our browsing as if we'd barely noticed the lanky gray-haired man in red suspenders working at a long table near the back. He would hoist a box of books to the surface and unpack it slowly, examining the dust jackets, flyleaves, copyright pages, sorting them according to the value he understood from a lifetime's study as a bibliophile. I think this is what most impressed me that day—the sight of Larry McMurtry working. He wasn't a star writer on a dais, behind a podium, on a film, but a mortal man enacting the kind of ranch-hand work ethic I'd grown up with, trundling those heavy boxes, hoisting, lifting, sorting. However much some may romanticize the writer's life, or the cowboy's life, the code for both is the same: work hard at hard work.

Still, it took me a while to get up my nerve. I think if Steve hadn't been there with his encouragement, and more particularly if I hadn't seen McMurtry working in such a way, maybe I never would have. I edged nearer. "Mr. McMurtry?" He glanced up. At once I saw an invisible shield drop down, a steely protectiveness. He didn't tell me to leave him alone, but his wariness and irritation were plain. I rattled off my rehearsed piece: in1992yougavemeawonderfulblurbformyfirst-bookstrangebusinessandIneverthankedyousoIjustwantedtosaythank-younowthankyousoverymuch. His expression eased. The protective wariness bled away. He didn't smile or become chatty and friendly, and I saw no sign that he recalled the book or the blurb or anything at all about *Strange Business*, but he seemed, if not warm, at least not offended, not invaded, and not impatient with me in any way. I don't remember what he said, or whether he said anything at all, actually— maybe he just nodded. But I felt acknowledged, as an individual, a fellow writer, and also maybe as someone who wasn't going to ask of him another damn thing. I smiled and backed away, and Larry McMurtry turned again to his work.

My heart was still pounding when I rejoined the others. Of the four of us, I think I was the most relieved and Steve the most pleased. Maybe it was, in a way, his thank-you, too. He'd read most of McMurtry's work—some twenty-three novels at that point, plus scores of nonfiction books, essays, reviews—and from the time he'd been introduced to *All My Friends Are Going to Be Strangers* by a friend in college, Steve had felt that, in a way no other writer's work had ever done, McMurtry's writing welcomed him home. Steve's family is from the same part of Texas as Clarendon, where Captain Call returns after his cattle drive in *Lonesome Dove*. The landscapes in McMurtry's fiction are Steve's landscapes, the historical characters in the novels live on in the oral history of Steve's family. It's a powerful bittersweet feeling, that kind of kinship, that shared ownership, when you come upon a writer who is writing your home territory. It's what I felt the first time I read the Choctaw/Welsh poet Jim Barnes—"You've got to leave this land again before it hurts / you into a sin the years will not ease"—writing about Summerfield, the little southeastern Oklahoma town where he grew up, a dozen miles across the muddy Fourche Maline from my grandfather's land. It's not always place, of course, where a writer strikes your heart; it can be a sensibility, a secret yearning, lust, the hidden eyes you see with, a writer writing your lost childhood. Your dreams.

I felt giddy, relieved of a great unacknowledged tension, as we lined up at the counter to pay for our books. Paul had found that rare book of poems by his friend Grandin—where else but in a town of half a million books might you find the single pearl you seek?—and I had collected a pile of histories about Tudor England and early-day Oklahoma. Connie and Steve each had their own tall, tidy stacks of treasures, and we paid for them all and walked back outside into the sweltering, slanting sunlight.

But what does this have to do with the things I want to write about? With history lived and denied, with torture and bad wars and the journalist James Foley and bearing witness to a world falling apart? Well, because it happened, just this way. That the narrative should begin with such an iconic American writer makes sense beyond any way I might have tried to orchestrate it. McMurtry's writings are laced through with references to Geronimo; he's tried as hard as any white writer since Angie Debo to tell the story from the Apache point of view—though in the end, of course, he fails, as we all fail, because white eyes can see only what they can see. But he has tried. And a certain debt was paid that day. And it happened on the same time continuum, that same pallid and searing August road trip, when we tried to see Geronimo's grave. It's part of the story in the way the story is always telling itself, not as a crazy quilt or mosaic, but as a sequential narrative of juxtaposition and coincidence, of time and place and events strung together, one after the other, in a spiral, a river, an unending flow.

So, yes, we left Archer City before sunset on a lingering prairie evening when the whitened August sky seemed to stay light forever. Connie rode with me so we could talk, and Paul and Steve rode in their car so they could do the same, the four of us talking and talking, the way we always talked, on the long drive back north across the Red River to Connie's home territory in the Wichita Mountains near Fort Sill.

Connie is an army brat; she grew up in Germany, North Carolina, Tennessee, but her teen years were spent in Lawton, those significant years of chaos and becoming, and so the place claimed her, or she claimed it, for her hometown. Like many western Oklahoma towns, Lawton was founded by the auctioning of Indian lands divided into town lots, a legal theft that began in Lawton on August 6, 1901. One hundred years before the evening we drove into town on Cache Road. Not that I knew this then, nor would I have thought much of it if I had known—the seductive, ungovernable power of coincidence wasn't yet a thread in our ongoing conversation, mine and Connie's. And we did not know what was coming. I recall no sign of a centennial celebration that night. Maybe an army town with its constant turnover and migration, its myriad soldiers and their families passing through, has, like America itself, little memory of how it actually came to be. Or maybe they celebrated and we just didn't see.

What I did see was an ordinary-looking army base town. Fast food. Neon lights. Pawn & Gun. Lawton could be located anywhere, I thought. Most towns in Oklahoma are so quirky and specific in their character that it seems to me they could only have sprung up here: Tahlequah, Okemah, Pawhuska, Anadarko—these have to be Oklahoma towns. Lawton, though, could be packed up and shipped to Georgia, New Jersey, California, Virginia, with little hint of disruption. Or so I was thinking as we cruised Cache Road, found a nice generic corporate hotel in which to spend the night, headed out next morning for breakfast at IHOP.

In bright early morning sunlight, we sat in the same restaurant where Connie and her friends used to come for coffee late at night. Same pink and orange décor, same sticky syrup pourers you'd find in any International House of Pancakes anywhere, but imbued for Connie with memory and weight. I tried to see the place through her eyes, but it seemed too generic to me. At the same time, it felt different from other such places in Oklahoma. The customers were more racially mixed, for one thing, their accents more varied; they were overall younger, and more of them were male. There's a kind of drawling, neighborly, geriatric friendliness you'll find amidst the pale skins and gray heads in the Shawnee IHOP or the one in Muskogee. But I felt a harder edge here, a hint of protective distance, something akin to the invisible wall that had dropped between Mr. McMurtry and me. These folks were all strangers. There was no natural neighborliness, no unspoken sense of *we're all in this together.* I was looking to find Connie's home territory, the place she writes from, but so far the town seemed bland and unfamiliar, too ordinary to be a force for fiction. But, of course (and I knew this even then), ugliness, beauty, story-worthy pain: they're always in the eyes of the one who sees.

Later we headed north, out of town, toward the Wichita Mountains.

Okay, I thought. This is why the place holds her.

One look, even at a great distance, and you feel it—this is an ancient place, outside history. Strange, craggy pyramids thrust up from the plains, not smoky blue from far off, as wooded mountains are, but umber and glowing. The crests are capped by five-hundred-million-year-old granite, creviced and rounded by eons of weather, with rivers of boulders tumbling down their slopes and a sea of mixed short and tall grasses all around: buffalo grass and grama, Indian grass and bluestem. The plains are khaki colored in August, dotted with bison, elk, deer, longhorn cattle, black-tailed prairie dogs: residents of the oldest managed wildlife preserve in the nation. The Wichita Mountains National Wildlife Refuge was established by Teddy Roosevelt in the years after the buffalo vanished. The plains bison, also known as American buffalo, didn't disappear by accident—they were systematically exterminated through U.S. government policy aided by greedy buffalo hunters with their Sharps rifles and immunity to waste.

It's such an American story: annihilate the native species, extermi-
nate them from their homelands, and then set up a park, and a federal
agency to administer it, to preserve that vanishing breed by shipping
fifteen survivors—six bulls and nine cows—in railcars halfway across
the country from New York. That happened in 1907, the year Oklahoma
became a state. In Lawton, an aging Quanah Parker and other Comanche elders met the train, old men for whom the buffalo hunt was not
some mythic past but living memory. By then free-roaming buffalo
had been gone from the southern plains for thirty years.

But what power the land holds, what memory. I was thinking
this as we entered the preserve on the back roads: how very different
Connie's Oklahoma is from mine. Both belong absolutely to the same
complex and complicated state we're both writing from, both have
their origination stories seeded in tragedy and violence and hope and
migration, yet they look and feel as different, well, as the east is from
the west. I grew up in Indian Territory, present-day eastern Oklahoma:
forest green in its essence, thickly wooded in most places, obscured
by shade and shadow and rolling, humpbacked hills. The tribes whose
stories I grew up with are the mighty Osage and the great southern
peoples, the Choctaw, Chickasaw, Cherokee, Creek, and Seminole,
removed from their homelands in the American South and marched
west in the early 1800s—a mere eyeblink on the spiral in comparison to
the ancient belonging of the plains tribes here in the old Comancheria,
the southwestern corner of Oklahoma Territory where Connie was
raised. This place, as I saw it that day, is dusty tan and pale blue in its
essence, the hues of sweeping plains and endless sky. The tribes here
are the Comanche and Kiowa and Arapaho: powerful horse-riding
roving peoples corralled at the end of the nineteenth century from
their vast territories onto small reservations in and around Fort Sill.
Soon the Apaches, including their warrior leader Geronimo, were
forced from their home in the western deserts, first to the swamplands
of Florida, and then to the lowlands of Alabama, where they had to
climb trees to see the sun and died in droves, and then here, to live as
prisoners of war inside the fort. The Kiowas have long held certain sites
in the Wichitas sacred. Rainy Mountain, for one. Longhorn Mountain,
for another—the western reaches of which private landowners have of
late leased to a private mining company to blast the native limestone

into gravel and truck it away: a twenty-first-century manifestation of our long history of desecration.

Desecration is what it seems to me, not sacrilege, for the land is sacred, not holy—a distinction I understand emotionally but cannot articulate. My upbringing, steeped as it was in evangelical Protestantism with its theological disdain for sacrament and ritual, runs up against the sensibilities of my Catholic-raised husband, for whom the power of sacrament has endured long past a childhood of catechism and weekly Mass, and the wordless influence of Indian friends, for whom ceremony is sacred, enduring, not to be spoken about. I have read that the Kiowa people go to Longhorn Mountain to gather cedar for ceremony. They go there to pray. There is no church, no outside religion. The land is sacred, not holy. And yet there's a compound on the preserve called the Holy City, a miniature first-century Palestine village nestled on the plains. That sort of incongruity is the very essence of this state.

The Holy City of the Wichitas was the first location Connie took us to that morning. It's the site of the longest-running Passion Play in America. In its 1930s heyday, crowds of three hundred thousand would attend the Easter performances that ran from dusk till dawn. I had visited the setting in Connie's fiction, was prepared for the incongruity, but not, I think, for how accidentally comical it seemed. We parked in the nearly empty parking lot and wandered along stone pathways past watchtowers and rock shrines and perimeter walls all built of locally quarried granite in the 1930s by the WPA. The little rock buildings were labeled Herod's Court, Pilate's Judgment Hall, the Lord's Supper Building, Mary and Martha's House. We made jokes about the pile of rocks boasting a hand-lettered sign that read "Tomb of Lazerus" (surely an unintentional misspelling), and the one labeled "Bethlehem Inn," which held on its reverse side a hand-drawn nativity scene complete with plywood cutouts of Mary and Joseph and the Baby Jesus in a manger. I was amused, and yet taken by how strange and hokey and simultaneously beautiful it seemed.

I remember sun and sweat and laughter, a high, rough prairie wind blowing, hot enough to take your breath away. We came to an elongated stone structure, perhaps three hundred yards wide and maybe fifteen feet tall, with various performance spaces at different heights where most of the Passion Play would be staged. I climbed the rocks, stood at the crest where the actor playing Jesus would ... what? Change the water into wine. Feed the multitudes. Throw the money changers out of the temple. Bear his cross, stumbling and beaten, toward the torture at Golgotha. I held the whipping hair out of my eyes, gazed out at the burning landscape, the craggy skull-like hills framing the horizon. I thought, yes, you could believe you are in ancient Palestine. An uneasiness nicked at me. Every faux setting here, every cornily labeled pile of rocks, had a matching story in my memory, etched there by the colored drawings in my Youth Bible, confirmed in the poetic syntax of King James. The discomfort I felt then was no more than a vague apprehension, an uncomfortable sense that to make jokes about this little mini–Holy Land was also, in some inherent way, to blaspheme. To blaspheme is to suffer punishment. *Thou shalt not. Thou shalt not.* The Bible tells me so.

Not that I said anything about this to the others, or even allowed the thoughts fully into my conscious mind. But I was glad when we began to saunter toward the parking lot in the late morning heat. The sun was high by the time we left the Holy City.

We drove on, winding our way to the top of Mount Scott, up and up and up along the long spiraling drive like the spiral of memory; on our right, cascades of rounded boulders lay scattered down the sides of the mountain like granite waterfalls, and far below, glimpsed on certain turns, Lake Lawtonka was a bright glaze, like an eye set in miles of khaki plains. In the asphalt lot at the crest we got out of the car, stood gazing west. There were then no rows of distant white wind turbines marching off toward the horizon, nothing to mar the sight of ancient crags and khaki plains extending to world's end in a faint smoky haze—and the wind, dear God, the wind, a hot ceaseless furnace blowing hard up the face of the mountain. An unrelenting roar. Connie said the wind never stops there. After a while we descended, headed toward Medicine Park.

Of all the places Connie guided us to that day, this kitschy-cool turn-of-the-century resort town was the one she seemed most excited to show us. The place lives large in Connie's fiction:

eccentric, evocative, quirkily unique. It's a funky-looking place, one
that could only be itself, could only be here, in this particular spot
on the planet. For one thing, the ruddy granite cobblestones you see
everywhere are a geological phenomenon unique to this land. We
wound our way through the narrow streets, between cottages and
shops constructed of those cobblestones, the size of small cannon-
balls, stacked one on top of the other to create porch columns and
walls. The buildings look as if they were put together with a giant
child's Play-Doh hand-rolled into little orbs. I had never seen such a
thing before.

A beautiful stream flows through the town, cool and clear looking.
This is Medicine Creek, sacred to the indigenous peoples whose land
this is, for whom the meaning of the word "medicine" is so much
more powerful and complex than this paltry English translation of
their word can convey. In the early twentieth century, the creek was
dammed to create a small lake called Bath for the health and pleasure
of white tourists, who would trek across the prairie to this manmade
resort town. Bath Lake is harnessed by stone walkways, crossed by
a wooden footbridge, the entire area landscaped with shade trees,
a green oasis in the khaki desert. Even beside the trickling waters,
though, it was hot as hell. Paul took a photograph of Connie and
me standing in dappled shade, looking cool and happy, but what I
remember most is the dampness under my arms and on my face, how
hot and sticky it all was, how the prairie wind was totally useless in the
sweltering heat beneath the trees, and it seems to me that, even then,
my face looked worried.

We crossed the street, passed from scalding sunlight into the
cooler darkness of the Old Plantation Inn, musty and dim and, to my
mind, not clean enough to eat in—though we did eat there, and later
walked around the main rooms studying the historical photographs
tacked up on the walls. I didn't have the eyes to see the place the way
Connie could see it, with the magnifying power of memory, autobi-
ography, the swell of drama and imagination a fiction writer uses to
give heightened form to the real landscapes she writes about. We see
place with our hearts, with our child-mind; it's hard to translate our
real-world models for someone else. I've seen the disappointment in
readers' eyes when I've shown them the real church or jail yard or

landscapes I've written about. Once, in Oxford, Mississippi, William Faulkner's nephew Jimmy showed me and some other visitors the real house owned by the real woman who was the model for the title character in "A Rose for Emily." But the frame house Jimmy Faulkner showed us looked nothing like the grand home in my reader's imagination—it wasn't complicated or spooky or striking enough for Miss Emily. So it was with Connie and the Old Plantation Inn. When I read her fiction, I see the place the way she sees it, funky and unique, full of intrigue, secret passages, and history. That hot August day in 2001, the place appeared to me merely dark and smelly, and not ancient and rich with history. Just old.

As we were leaving town, we stopped at a little tourist shop down the road. This is my most enduring Medicine Park memory. The woman who owned the store told us that something weird was going on. The base was locked down, she said; no civilians could visit. That was unusual, Connie said. She'd spent her youth bopping onto the base to see her dad or show friends around. She had known the base to be closed for maneuvers from time to time; it wasn't unheard of, but it was rare. There seemed to be a kind of tension going around, the shopkeeper told us. An edginess she hadn't seen before. But America was pre-9/11 then; we still lived in our general cocooned sense of security, and soon enough, between Connie and the woman, the topic was dropped.

Inside my head, though, a silent little alarm was sounding. In my younger years this would happen whenever I saw a military convoy passing or, hearing the roar, looked up to see jets flying in formation overhead. It surely happened whenever the car radio squealed its test of the Emergency Broadcast System. In grade school we practiced surviving a nuclear attack by crouching beneath our metal desks with our hands clasped over our heads. On Wednesday nights my pastor railed from the pulpit with a newspaper in one hand, a King James Bible opened to the last book in the other, showing us the signs of the last days: earthquakes in diverse places, the moon turning to blood. Tribulation. The Four Horsemen of the Apocalypse. Armageddon. I was raised on Revelation at the height of the Cold War. I internalized my doomsday visions early. The fact is, I've been waiting for the end of the world all my life.

So when the woman in the tourist shop said that something strange was going on, I believed her. That's when the earlier uneasiness that had pricked at me gave way to a quiet foreboding. The sense of dread stayed with me as Paul and I bought a ceramic lizard and an openmouthed frog rain gauge to measure the biblical toad-strangler rainstorms we get in our part of the country. Nothing dramatic or out of the ordinary happened. We just went on. When we drew near Apache Gate, the entrance to Fort Sill that was on our way, we decided to try, despite what the tourist shop lady had told us, to get on base to see Geronimo's grave.

The exchange was brief—a soldier stepped out of a shaded kiosk into the hot sun to tell us the base was closed to visitors. All right, we'd tried. A little collective shrug. Steve turned the car around, and we headed back to the blacktop. A short while later, in Lawton, we said our goodbyes. Paul and I got in our car, and we all headed in our separate directions, and I forgot all about the foreboding. For a month and a few days.

On September 8, 2001, I was in Amherst, Massachusetts, at a back-to-school picnic for the MFA creative writing students at the University of Massachusetts, where I was to teach a fiction workshop that fall. The party was at the program director's home, burgers and hotdogs and beer on a beautiful New England autumn afternoon spilling into evening. I knew no one. They all knew each other, or so it felt to me as I wandered the grassy yard in my cowboy boots with my overfilled paper plate and plastic cup. The Visiting Stranger, that's been my role for most of the years I've been teaching, one familiar enough that it seemed to me completely normal to be the outsider at the party, genial and pleasant, I hoped, and very slightly detached: just there to teach a short while before returning to my separate writing life. I forget now who walked me around and introduced me to the students who would be in my workshop. One of the faculty members, I presume. Might have been one of the students.

"It is easy to see the beginnings of things," Joan Didion writes in "Goodbye to All That," "and harder to see the ends." But not always. Not when the end is so violent and public, repeated on horrific news loops around the world, and the beginning so peacefully ordinary.

They welcomed me with friendly remarks about how they were looking forward to the class. Nice, smart, articulate white kids, amiable and good-looking and kind. Not kids, actually; they were in their late twenties then, but they seemed young to me in their open-heartedness and enthusiasm. I remember the brilliance of the sky, the tree-shaded beauty of the afternoon, the fresh sense of possibility that the beginning of school brings. I'm sure I met most of the students that day, but the faces that come to me now are the four whose lives would intersect mine far beyond the reach of that exquisite world-shattering September. Shauna Seliy. Erin White. Brian Jordan. Jim Foley.

For me, the hardest thing about writing nonfiction is sketching character from the very real, complex people I know. No matter what I put down, it's never enough, and yet too much. How dare I describe what people look like, much less what they think, feel, believe? But here's how I first saw them: Shauna, diminutive and intense, her straight brown hair cut short and tucked back behind her ears, the keenness of her intellect held close beneath a kind of self-protectiveness. Erin, pretty, open-faced, brunette, with the glow, that weekend, of the newlywed. She told me she wished her wife, Chris, had come so I could meet her. Erin's warmth made me think of the kind of southern-style graciousness I knew from women back home, though she grew up, actually, in Colorado. None of them were southerners, in fact. Jim grew up in New Hampshire, not far from the Massachusetts border. Shauna's roots, as I learned from her fiction, go deep in the Pennsylvania coal-mining country. Brian is a "proud Jersey boy," as he once told me, born and bred. Tall and thin, with a high, elegant forehead, Brian has a measured way of talking, as if he's gauging his words to find the kindest way to put things. He has—they all have—the kind of generosity of spirit and decency that I think of as what's best in the American character. Jim had that, too. Absolutely. He was lively, good humored, handsome in that athletic all-American way, and he was a great kidder; he loved to goof around. You could see how much everyone liked him. It's hard not to imbue that first meeting with what I came to know later: Jim's seriousness of purpose, his moral depth, the way he held himself, energized, just a little off from the present moment, as if he had somewhere else he needed to go, some urgent job to do. But in truth, from that first meeting what I remember most is his friendliness, his thick shock of auburn-tinged brown hair, his engaging, slightly gap-toothed grin, and the fact there was a softball game or a volleyball game or some kind of participatory sports thing he was anxious to get to.

The next Monday evening, we had our first workshop. I don't remember whose stories we critiqued, which students talked most, or what was said; I have no idea whether the work was polished or sorely in need of revision. Even my recollection of where everyone sat around the long conference table—Jim and Shauna close beside each other and to my left, a kind of symmetry and connection I mistook for their being lovers at first, rather than what they were, extremely close friends—is in fact a melding of what I remember from the whole semester. That fiction workshop at UMass is one of the ones I remember most vividly from all my years of teaching, but its beginning, too, is blurred. I recall sensing a kind of woundedness in the air, an atmosphere of tentativeness or caution that I didn't understand, and I also recall recognizing straightaway what a strong workshop it was going to be, how serious and committed these young writers were.

That night after class, I got in my car and drove three hours to my home in the Catskills. I had a place to stay in Amherst, but I wanted to go home because I hadn't seen my husband for a few days. Next morning, as we sat together in our living room watching the smoke billow from the burning towers, I was glad I'd made the late-night drive, because we were able to share it together, that beginning, which of course I do remember, as we all remember, all of us who were alive and old enough to perceive it then—where we were, what we saw and felt and said. We all have our stories. I was talking on the phone with a friend; she said, "Did you see where a plane hit the World Trade Center?" I got off the phone, turned on the TV. By then the second plane had hit. I stood staring at the screen a moment and then hurried outside to my husband's writing studio to tell him. "Something terrible is happening," I said. "It's a war, I think. We're under attack." I remember us walking back across the yard on that glorious September morning, its colors all primary blue and butter yellow, to sit watching history unfold in real time, narrated in real time by the urgent voice of Peter Jennings, the tiny bodies falling, the surreal, dreamlike moment when the first tower fell, that impossible cloud of cascading dust.

Soon there was news of the Pentagon strike, Flight 93 going down in a field in Pennsylvania, and it was clear that what I'd said was true, we were under attack. We didn't know yet by whom—though bin Laden's name was already being bandied about on the news—or, most significant to me, *why*. I would spend much of that fall trying to understand the *why*, sitting at my computer poring over articles about al-Qaeda in Afghanistan, the radicalization of Osama bin Laden at the time of the Gulf War, the American embassy bombings in Kenya and Tanzania, the USS *Cole*, all of which I remembered from news accounts when they happened, none of which, except for the start of the Gulf War, had had any effect on me. And that's how we are with our history, isn't it? Most of us, anyway. Unless the unfolding touches us directly, cuts hard inside our protected lives, it's only dim and distant voices, an insect hum at the periphery.

When the towers fell, though, all I could think about was my godson's mother, Marlene, who worked not far from the Trade Center at Banco Popular. I called and called her family's house in Brooklyn, but the lines were jammed, *all circuits are busy, all circuits are busy,* and then finally only the buzzing rhythmic signal; there was no way to get a call into or out of the city that day. I tried to believe she was all right, but even from the distance at which the television cameras recorded the destruction, you could see how far it reached: all through downtown Manhattan. But there was nothing to be done, nothing we could do, except sit in front of the television and watch.

By early evening, when it seemed clear there would be no new information, no greater understanding, just the same repeated images—smoke billowing from the towers, the tumbling debris cloud, the jagged gash in the Pentagon—Paul turned off the TV. Then we were at terrible loose ends. We had no real appetite, no ability to cook or work or accomplish anything. We drove to a restaurant in White Lake just to do something, just to get out of the house. At Buster's, everyone was subdued, extraordinarily polite. Paul and I sat on the deck and looked at the lake, the light and weather too exquisite, too lovely, to bear so much tragedy. The waitress and the few other customers seemed to be going through the motions in a state of stunned silence. None of us spoke, at first, about the unspeakable. I remembered how, ten and a half years earlier, on January 17, 1991, I'd flown from New York to Tulsa on the morning the first Gulf War started. I remembered the eerie stillness at La Guardia, how strangers seemed hardly willing to look at one another, and how courteous we all were, waving one another ahead in line, while all around, on the televisions and the front pages of newspapers, blared the single word WAR. This evening in White Lake was like that. At length we had a brief exchange with another couple at a nearby table, but the event was too enormous. None of us had words. We shared the acknowledgment of what had happened essentially with gesture: shaking our heads. *We are all in this together.* I think now that the stunned sleepwalking look they wore was likely as much on my face, and on Paul's, as it was on theirs.

Later we drove over to the Woodstock site. A large concrete slab in the corner of Max Yasgur's old hayfield marks the memory of the 1969 festival: Three Days of Peace and Music in White Lake, New York. It's hard to explain how completely unsurprising it felt to see a group of friends and neighbors already gathered there. No word had gone out. We had all just come to that iconic site on our own, because we needed ritual, we needed the power of place to enact it. We needed, truth to tell, prayer, though none of us was comfortable to say so. We didn't have a church to go to, we couldn't drive down to New York, though I know many of us wanted to. There was no shared cultural ceremony for such a disaster. We did what we did spontaneously. Somebody had brought along a clutch of small American flags. They handed us each one, and we gathered in a silent circle around that concrete monument to peace and rock music from three decades before. After a while someone began to sing "God Bless America," and we all joined in. I'm surprised to realize how quickly, and without coordination, that happened, and how, without much thought, Paul and I took part in the flag waving and "God Bless America" singing that would become the ubiquitous national response to 9/11.

When the students and I came back together in Amherst the following Monday, the world had changed. America was a new country, at once meaner and kinder, more suspicious and more unified, wounded and scarred and less free than any America we'd known before, and barreling headlong, though we didn't fully know it yet, toward war. Who can write fiction when the very real, urgent, present world is falling apart? It would be the journalists, of course, who'd first chronicle the story, followed soon by the poets, and finally, years later, the novelists would begin to bring forth works set in a post-apocalyptic New York, a changed nation; it just takes that long for fiction. We were all struggling that fall. I was. In October a writer friend told me that Joyce Carol Oates had told him she was having a hard time writing in the wake of the attacks, and I thought, God, if Joyce Carol Oates can't write, no wonder none of the rest of us can. But we were in a fiction workshop, and stories and novels were the demands of the class, and anyway, what else does one do when the world is falling apart but go to work? And so we did.

A bond was forged between several of us in that workshop. We were like survivors. We'd gone through this searing experience, at once public and personal, that had nothing to do with any of us individually but everything to do with the whole of us. National history had broken in, created a distinct *Before* and *After,* which they, being of the last generation to come to young adulthood in the *Before*, understood acutely. There was a shared commitment to the cause of fiction—we were all in some sense true believers—and there was, above all, in my memory, at least, the extraordinary ordinary decency of those young writers, the truth of how hard they worked, how intuitively kind they were, and how, in myriad ways, their fiction aspired to those humane qualities Faulkner talked about: love and honor and pity and pride and compassion and sacrifice. The world knows now, because of how his story has been told and retold, how fundamental these attributes were to Jim Foley's character, how, when he was in the worst extremities of torture and deprivation under ISIS, he exhibited just such honor and sacrifice, but that's not my story to tell, except to say that it was there already, years before, in the months after 9/11. You could see it in the thread of conscience in his fiction, feel it in the careful, supportive feedback he gave the other writers. He was only in his twenties then, but you could feel the integrity in him, the sense that he believed he had a responsibility to make the world better. But the thing is, it wasn't just Jim. This strength of character, this *heart*, was there in the others as well. And the world tumbled on, and U.S. warplanes began bombing

Afghanistan, and in America people were dying of anthrax, infinitesimal particles of poison puffed into the air from envelopes sent through the mails, and in December, during the Battle of Tora Bora, Osama bin Laden escaped to Pakistan. Every day in the news there was talk of terrorism and fear, but in our workshop those young writers had not forgotten the problems of the human heart in conflict with itself, as Faulkner worried about in his Nobel speech. The human heart in conflict with itself was the very woof and weave of their stories.

And then the semester ended and I left Amherst, returned to my Catskills cabin in deep winter and tried and tried to write. I was working on *Harpsong* then, struggling to carry my mind back to drought-ridden, dust-choked Oklahoma in the 1930s. But the world was too much with me. I spent hours at my computer, poring over news stories, trying to understand where the al-Qaeda attacks had come from: why did they hate us so much as to take all those innocent and unoffending lives? I thought of what happened that day to Marlene. The bank where she worked was only blocks from the World Trade Center, and while the planes were still burning and the smoke billowing and the bodies falling into the streets, Marlene and her coworkers fled their building; she was making her way east toward the river when the first tower fell. She had to run and run, she said, trying to escape that devastating rain of debris and boiling, choking dust, and finally she took refuge along with a few others in an unnamed office building in the midst of that great deluge; she hid beneath a desk in almost total darkness, she said, and could not breathe, and outside the sirens screamed and screamed. Then the second tower fell, and Marlene believed there was no escape; she thought she was going to die. There was no way to call her family to tell them she was alive now, or that she might soon not be, no way to tell her mother and son and husband goodbye. Hours later, Marlene and the others hiding with her emerged to an apocalyptic nightmare; there were still no phone lines from which to call, no subway service, no transportation. She started walking, along with thousands of others, east across the Brooklyn Bridge, toward home.

How long had it been before I finally reached Marlene and learned what she'd gone through? A day and a half, I think. How long before I drove to Brooklyn to see her and Travis? I don't know.

I can't remember. My godson was only eleven then, not old enough to understand, really, what had happened, but plenty old enough to suffer the trauma his whole family suffered in the hours it took Marlene to walk home across the Brooklyn Bridge. On his tenth birthday, I had taken him to the top of the World Trade Center to celebrate. We talked about that later—how glad we were to have been there at least once. But those moments of reassurance and grace don't stand alone as beads on the spiral of memory for me; they have no specific relation to other events, no distinction, and so I know they happened, I can hear Marlene's voice on the phone saying, "I thought I was going to die," but that moment falls into the gray space between events. As does the time I called Connie from New York—when was it? Weeks after 9/11? A month? "But we knew, Connie," I said. "Remember? Or somebody knew. Remember how the base was closed that day when we tried to go there, and the woman at the gift shop thought it was so weird?"

"Oh, right, that's right," Connie said, but she didn't seem as bothered by the recollection as I felt. "It's not all that weird, though. They used to close for maneuvers and stuff when I was a kid. It might not have had anything to do with those warnings."

"But it might."

"I don't know."

Well, we don't know, do we? We'll never know. *Maybe it's just me*, I thought. Seeing secrets hidden in every sign. But I couldn't shake the sense of foreboding I'd had that day, the cold feel of dread. *And there shall be wars and rumors of wars . . .*

One blustery cold weekend in March, three months after our workshop ended, those four students, Brian, Erin, Shauna, and Jim, drove over from Amherst to my place in the Catskills for a writers' weekend. They brought loads of food and a little beer and their hunger to be better writers. We all shared our work. I wasn't workshop leader then, but just another writer among them. I remember very well the fiction they were working on. Jim's was a novel based on the students from his years teaching in an impoverished area of Phoenix. I remember how we had to keep a fire going in the woodstove, how crowded we were, the four of them camped out on the sofa bed and bedrolls on the floor. I think that weekend is when I first understood there was an enduring connection between us, not just the kind of authentic but ephemeral community I'd been used to in workshops. I see them all wrapped in scarves and hats, Jim in a huge oversized parka, as they trooped outside for a wintry walk in the Catskill woods. Four young writers on the brink of their lives. Everything was possible. One moment stays with me: in the cramped quarters of the cabin, Jim brushed against a shelf and knocked a glass vase to the floor. The vase meant nothing, but his apologies were huge and heartfelt, outsized for the size of the transgression. Something about that memory makes me ache—the acute responsibility he felt. Jim didn't stay for the full weekend; he had to leave early for a prior commitment. Even then he had someplace else he had to be.

It was the following winter, in the run-up to the invasion of Iraq, that my husband and I joined an activist peace group in our county and united with tens of thousands of others marching in Washington and New York. In Massachusetts, Jim and the others were also marching, protesting, hoping to prevent this new war from starting. In LeAnne Howe's novel *Shell Shaker* there's the oft-repeated phrase "You cannot stop what is coming." Ominous, terrifying in its way. And of course we cannot stop what is coming, but we also cannot see it; we don't know until the story ends what parts will turn out to have been relative, orchestrated, which merely incidental.

Scroll forward a decade to a hot, windy afternoon in late April 2011. My friend Connie Squires and I are back at Fort Sill, and once again she's looking to take me to see Geronimo's grave. The country is different now; we know things we didn't know ten years ago. We have images: a black-hooded prisoner at Abu Ghraib standing on a box with electric wires attached to his fingers; a young female GI holding a dog leash lashed around the neck of a naked Iraqi prisoner lying on the floor; and that same young white soldier and her khaki-clad male colleague standing behind a pyramid of stacked naked prisoners proudly giving a thumbs-up sign. Enhanced interrogation is part of our national lexicon, and whatever was unleashed that crystal-blue

September morning in 2001, it's part of the everydayness of what it means to be American now.

But this day Connie and I aren't studying the world's troubles. We're talking fiction, talking work—I'm back teaching with her again in Edmond—and our friendship is ten years deeper, and the power of place that compels each of as writers is understood by the other in the language of source and craft. I'm nearing the end of writing *Kind of Kin,* a novel grounded in my home territory of southeastern Oklahoma, and Connie is working on *Live from Medicine Park,* set here in this very landscape where we're traveling, and the day is glorious, warm with the promise of summer, delectably perfect—except for the wind, that high, hot southern plains wind thundering north from Texas, ceaseless, heartless, whipping our hair into our mouths and eyes as we stand beside her car to take a picture outside Meers Store. But the sweat and windy outdoor smell, they're immaterial; we're just glad to be on a road trip together. We eat our longhorn burgers in the musty cluttered coolness of Meers Store and Restaurant, saunter back outside to the wind and squinty sunlight, and climb in her car to drive over to Fort Sill. Once again we approach Apache Gate, once again we stop at the kiosk to explain ourselves, and this time—no problem—the soldier waves us through.

Connie drives slowly as we cruise past red-tile-roofed barracks, their buff-yellow walls bouncing sunlight so that I feel that I'm not so much in Oklahoma but in the great American Southwest—Spanish architecture, desert light—and I wonder at the order and aesthetic and size of the place. Connie tells me Fort Sill is where the Army's field and air defense artillery schools are located, where more than a quarter of American soldiers get their basic combat training, and I think, *Yeah, that makes sense.* When I meet people in other parts of the country, often all they know of Oklahoma is Lawton and Fort Sill, and that's because they came here for boot camp. None of them has ever mentioned what the base looks like, though. I'd expected drab gray barracks, a concrete fortress, not this rolling campus of landscaped grounds laced with gently curving roads and, dotted here and there, antique cannons and artillery guns enshrined like public art.

"I had no idea it was so beautiful," I say.

Connie nods. "And expensive. People don't realize the enormous cost of keeping a standing army." And I realize, a little mortified, that I've never thought of that before. For all my antiwar protesting, from walking around campus at Oklahoma Baptist University in 1969 wearing a black armband during the Vietnam Moratorium to the huge multi-thousands Iraq War marches in D.C. and New York in 2003, I've never once thought about an alternative to the way our nation keeps vast forces of men and weapons standing ready for war, even in peacetime. Then I ask myself, *What peace? How often have we been truly at peace in my lifetime?* Connie points to a building: "That's where I used to go to get my braces tightened." And, a bit later: "There's the commissary where I used to hang out and wait for my dad." And I'm struck again, as I have been many times in our years of friendship, by the disparity between our experiences growing up in Oklahoma— Connie's military-forged youth in Lawton and my mundane childhood in Bartlesville—and yet our lives have both been shaped by war. I grew up in the shadow of the "good" war, World War II, believing one thing about America, and in the hot midst of the "bad" one, Vietnam, believing something entirely different. Connie grew up in the aftermath of the bad war—her dad was a Vietnam vet—and was still young when he left to serve in the first Gulf War in 1991. Both of us have been shaped by the invisible forces of the Cold War: me hiding beneath my desk in grade school, Connie living in a divided Germany in the years before the Berlin Wall came down. From her car window, I gaze out at passing soldiers in desert fatigues, the many military vehicles, all kinds of bustling activity everywhere, but there's no sense of urgency; it's just business as usual. If you didn't know we were at war, you wouldn't think it from driving through here. But that's the unremarkable condition of America now, this state of perpetual war that most of us don't think about because it doesn't impact our lives directly, only the lives of soldiers and their families. This is what we believe.

The media tell us, if they mention it at all, that we're fighting the longest war in U.S. history. That's because they don't count the three hundred years of the Indian Wars, which began in 1622 with colonists making war on the Powhatan Confederacy and lasted until the final Apache raid inside U.S. borders in 1924. The Indian Wars are truly our longest legacy of warfare, but of course, those were undeclared wars. But then, so was Vietnam. So are the ones we're fighting in

Afghanistan and Iraq on this day in 2011, with seemingly no end in sight, though our current president has promised to end the "wrong" war in Iraq, so that we might concentrate on and win the "right" one in Afghanistan. Bad wars, good wars, wrong wars, right wars, I'm stunned, still, by the handsomeness of this place, with its uniformity and carefully tended lawns and red Spanish tiles and pale buildings and smooth curving roadways snaking along.

We pass the old guardhouse where Geronimo was kept prisoner, the regal three-story eminence of post headquarters with its giant American flag jutting straight out in the wind, drive through the Old Post Quadrangle. Connie tells me that when she was a kid, everyone wanted to live here. It was like a badge of prestige, she says, to live in historic housing dating back to when the fort was built. The Indian Territory fort I've been most familiar with is Fort Gibson, just north of Muskogee, but that built-in-a-square fortress with its cramped log barracks and tiny windows, preserved now as a National Historic Site, feels so much more primitive than this place. Edging the quadrangle are a number of pale stone houses with screened porches: handsome, elegant, aged. We pass a small, squat-steepled stone chapel, and then Connie points to a building. "Someone told me that's where the Kiowa warrior Sitting Bear was housed. They put him in a wagon to take him to prison, and they say he covered his head with a blanket and gnawed deep into the skin of his own wrists to slip out of his shackles. Then he started singing his death song. He told a bystander, 'See that tree? When I reach that tree, I will be dead,' and grabbed a soldier's carbine, and of course they shot him dead—a suicide by cop kind of move." I watch the old stone building as we drive slowly past it, but the façade reveals nothing. You have to know the story. That's the violent power of this place, I think, this fortress built for war, despite all its aesthetic handsomeness: raised up out of the southern plains to house U.S. Cavalry to fight Indians, headquarters for the famed Buffalo Soldiers, burial site of Kiowa chief Satanta and Comanche leader Quanah Parker and the great Apache legend Geronimo.

And that's where we go now. The Apache cemetery is located well outside the main area, at the end of one of the long, snaking roads. Connie parks in the lot, where a few other nonmilitary cars are scattered about, and we walk through a gate, amble slowly in humid shade beneath a long copse of cedars toward the grave. What did I expect, all these years we've talked about visiting Geronimo's grave? I don't know. Certainly not what I find, this pyramid of ruddy cobblestones stacked and bound with concrete, centered with a pale cement plaque spelling out in carved concrete letters GERONIMO, and crowned with a blunt, stylized concrete eagle with spreading wings. Below the pyramid, a flat flagstone rectangle marks the place where I assume the bones of the great warrior lie at rest. Colorful kerchiefs hang from the trees: Apache prayer cloths. A strange menagerie of tokens and talismans are laid about the monument itself, keychains, folded dollar bills, frayed business cards—whatever, I suppose, visitors had in their pockets and handbags when they came—but also things that seem to have been brought with intention. Dreamcatchers. Fading plastic flowers. The gifts remind me of the teddy bears and ribbons and car tags decorating the fence outside the Oklahoma City Bombing Memorial, that spontaneous outpouring of gifts at the site of a public tragedy preserved today as a tourist attraction. There are other white visitors in the cemetery, walking the paths, reading the headstones of the Apache dead: uniform pale stone markers that all look exactly the same. Created by the U.S. military, not Apache families. I think of a hot afternoon years ago when I went with two Indian friends to visit their mother's grave near Bristow. She'd been gone since winter. There was no headstone. The grave was overgrown with sumac and tall grasses. One of the brothers took out his pack of cigarettes, tore the filter off one, opened the white paper, and sprinkled the tobacco on his mother's resting place: an offering. He pocketed the filter and paper. Only the tiny brown flecks of tobacco sprinkled among the grasses remained.

I'm not surprised to see other visitors here. I know how powerful Geronimo's name is in our national narrative: a name to be both admired and feared. A cunning and fearless warrior, nearly mythological in his unconquerable nature, Geronimo and his small band of a few dozen Apaches eluded U.S. Cavalry troops for years. At one point nearly a quarter of the U.S. Army's forces—some five thousand men—were trying to capture him. Geronimo was the last Indian warrior to surrender; his name stands in the American mythos for both hero and enemy, the epitome of all that is undefeatable in the

American character, all that remains unconquerable, untamable, in the American West. But I've read Angie Debo's *Geronimo: The Man, His Time, His Place.* I know how much more tragic and complicated and slyly comical than the legend Geronimo's story is. I know he did not ride his horse off a cliff at Medicine Bluff to escape capture by U.S. soldiers, though that part of the legend is why parachutists call out his name as they jump. That myth is so ubiquitous and inescapable that when I was a kid climbing around in the rafters of new houses under construction in my neighborhood, I'd spit over the side of a rafter and cry out "Geronimooooooo!" as the spit hurled through the air to land with a satisfying splat on the concrete below.

I've got a different consciousness now. I'm suddenly uncomfortable. I don't want to feel like a tourist. It's not as if I feel it's a sacrilege to be here—all these keychains and ribbons, they're no desecration. I grew up with the southerners' habit of visiting cemeteries often, decorating our graves, bringing flowers and tokens to honor our dead. But something about being here feels voyeuristic to me, or—I don't know. Too close to the cultural appropriation I worry about and dread. Still, I ask one of the wandering visitors to take a photo of Connie and me beside the cobblestone pyramid. Connie's strawberry blond hair is lifted and tossed about, and my face in the photograph, when I see it later, appears blurry, soft and weak looking in the buffeting wind. It's the last Friday in April, just days before my favorite month is upon us, that month of greening warmth with its "mild May dust," as Faulkner called it. There's nothing mild about the spitting, stinging dust this day. I'm worn and sweaty, and something doesn't feel right. Connie and I wander back along the shaded path to her Honda.

On the drive back to Edmond, Connie tells me about a scene she's writing for her novel that's set at Geronimo's grave, and our conversation segues to the time, years before, when we tried to visit just a day after George W. Bush received the intelligence briefing warning that bin Laden meant to attack on American soil. Then she tells me a story I've never heard, about how Bush's grandpa, Prescott Bush, was among a party of Yalies serving at Fort Sill during World War I; they dug up Geronimo's grave, stole his skull and some bones and a few pieces of horse tack that had been buried with him, and carried them back to New Haven, where they enshrined them as relics in the tomblike structure that housed their secret student society, Skull and Bones—the same secret society that his grandson George W., the president who got us into the Iraq War, had been a member of, too. Connie said that supposedly the skull was still there, inside a glass case, or anyway, somebody's skull was there, and the Skull and Bones members all called it Geronimo.

"No kidding?" I say. "Is that true?"

"I don't know. They say it is."

"You mean Geronimo's skull is in Connecticut? Not under the stones where we just visited his grave?"

Connie shakes her head, eyes on the highway. "Who knows?"

And I'm thinking not only what a sacrilege that is, to steal the great warrior's bones, but also how weird, that sort of symmetry, that weird interconnectedness, Bush and Bush and Geronimo's grave and our two journeys to go there in these years of wars and rumors of wars. But then I'm always looking for the connectedness in things, cohesion, some kind of invisible orchestration. "Charles Dickens said it, you know," I offer. "When people criticized all the coincidences in his novels, he said we are all so much more connected than we could ever believe."

Our conversation segues then to narrative and coincidence and how difficult it is to fold coincidence into fiction, even when it's based on events that really happened, because modern readers won't stand for it. They're too skeptical. They don't like to see the creator's orchestrating hand. We may believe in chaos theory, that the flutter of a butterfly's wings halfway around the world can change a tornado's path in Oklahoma, but we don't believe in coincidence. Then Connie tells me another story: about how she met an old army vet at a bar in Norman, and how, after they got to talking, she learned that he had served with her dad at Fort Sill, but beyond that, he had taken over her father's duty to lead an army exercise one day—this was well before Connie was born—so her dad could take his fiancée, Connie's future mom, to meet his family in Texas; and how that exercise cost the guy his career, because it was a mock ambush, and somehow the trainees used live ammo instead of dummy ammo, leaving two Fort Sill GIs dead and this guy's life in shambles. Connie says she keeps trying to write about it in fiction, but the accidental meeting when she ran into the guy comes out seeming too coincidental. But that chance meeting is so much a part of the story. To tell it without that element bleeds the narrative too much away from the story she wants to write. "You might think about writing it as nonfiction," I tell her. "I think readers accept coincidence in life better than they do in fiction."

Our trip to Geronimo's grave took place on April 29, 2011. Twenty-five days earlier, my friend Jim Foley and two other journalists, Clare Morgana Gillis and Manu Brabo, had been taken prisoner by Muammar Qaddafi's forces in Libya, and a photojournalist traveling with them, Anton Hammerl, was killed. Jim and the others were still being held captive. I knew he had been taken—our friend Brian, who always kept me apprised of what Jim was up to, had emailed me—and I was concerned, of course, worried, as everyone who knew Jim was worried, but I can't say, looking back, that the thought of Jim Foley was with me that day. Connie and I parted ways in Edmond, and the next morning I drove back to my home near McAlester. The following night, Sunday, May 1, at 11:35 P.M., President Obama came on the news to announce that Osama bin Laden had been killed by U.S. forces in Pakistan.

Early Monday morning I called Connie. "You heard?"

"Amazing, isn't it?" she said, and what was unspoken between us was the knowledge shooting back and forth of everything we'd talked about on our road trip, the strangeness of simultaneity, that August 6, 2001, intelligence briefing: "Bin Laden Determined to Strike in US."

I said, "You know what his code name was, right?"

"No, what?"

"Geronimo."

A moment of marveling silence, then our conversation spiraled once again around coincidence, synergism, invisible connections, what, if anything, it all might mean. Later, following protests from Geronimo's family, U.S. officials would try to clarify that Geronimo was the code name not for bin Laden himself, but for that phase of the operation when he was slain. A, B, C, D, E, F, G: Geronimo. Still, what the world knew from news reports was that the SEAL team leader radioed bin Laden's death back to the White House by saying: "For God and country—Geronimo, Geronimo, Geronimo." And when he was prompted by a general for confirmation, he said, "Geronimo E.K.I.A."

Enemy Killed in Action.

Sixteen days later, Jim Foley and his fellow captives in Libya were released. Jim came back to the States. He visited Shauna in Chicago. They had a special bond, the two of them, begun those years ago in Amherst; there's a wonderful photo from that visit of Jim making goofy smiling faces with her toddler son. He gave a famous talk at Marquette University, where he spoke of the need for journalists to tell the true stories of war, about the need for moral courage. And then he went back to the war zone to continue telling those stories. On Thanksgiving Day, November 22, 2012, in Syria, James Foley was taken captive again.

How could this be part of the story, I wondered, that Jim would be kidnapped in a war zone not once but twice? It seemed too unbelievable. The narrative had too much . . . what? Coincidence. Too much orchestration. For days, and then weeks, and then months, there was no information about who'd taken him, where he was being held, whether he was alive or dead. I kept up with what was known—or, more accurately, not known—through Facebook, and also through emails from Brian, who lived in Boston and was privy to the private layers of rumor and the anguished searching Jim's family was going through. And then it was spring, and still no word, and then summer, the seasons turning in their elliptical spiral. And then it was Thanksgiving again, and Jim had been gone for over a year. I learned from Brian that Jim's parents, John and Diane, felt they could not say many things publicly out of fear for Jim's safety. I learned they were gathering money to continue their private search for him, without aid from the U.S. government—all that is public knowledge now. What is not public is how I thought sometimes, during the nearly two years of Jim's captivity: how I prayed he was alive, as many did; prayed for his safety, his safe return. I wanted to believe that, somehow, because of Jim's character, because of who he was, the worst kinds of horrors were not being visited upon him. But the images of tortured Iraqi prisoners at Abu Ghraib haunted me. I knew that whoever was holding Jim was likely doing the same kinds of things to him—and worse. Sometimes it was so painful to think of how he must be suffering that I wondered if I should be praying he was still alive. Sometimes I thought, *maybe what Jim's going through is worse than death.* But I couldn't hold those thoughts for long—the hope that there was an unknown miracle of grace happening for him was too strong. Then, in late spring 2014, I got an email from Brian: Jim was alive! His family had received proof; there was movement, Brian couldn't tell me what—it all had to be kept under the radar, only passed among us by word of mouth or private message—because whoever was holding Jim had threatened to kill him if negotiations were made public. But, oh yes, even so, there was reason to hope.

At that time, news of the wars in Syria and Iraq, and all through that part of the world, had receded to a dim rumble at the edge of my hearing. My parents were getting older, more frail, more forgetful; they needed more help. I'd begun a frequent shuttling back and forth between New York and Oklahoma. On August 19, I flew home for an extended visit to help take care of my mom and dad. My sister Ruth picked me up at the airport. On the ride back to Red Oak, I turned on my phone to check messages; there was a Facebook message from my niece Faith: "Rilla, is this your friend?" and a photograph of Jim's face. The headline read: "American Journalist Executed." I cried out, threw the phone onto the floorboard as if it were the thing that had hurt him, hurt me. I didn't want to pick it up again to read the news, but I had to. My sister kept saying, "What? Rilla, what is it?" but for the longest time I just kept shaking my head, reading, crying. I couldn't talk.

It was maybe forty minutes later, standing in my mother's living room, that I got the first phone call. I knew it was Shauna, her name flashing on my phone's caller ID. At first there was only silence. Then I heard her choked sobbing. I think I said, "I know," and then we were both crying. I don't remember if we said anything after that. I guess we did. I can't remember any words, just our weeping and the powerful feel of connection across all that time and distance. It was the same later when I talked with Erin and Brian. We reached out, the four of us, by phone and email and text message, sharing our private loss in the midst of that vast public news. Each of us had to choose what we would let in of the horror repeated so constantly, and by what means we would receive it, though I had little choice because my mother always kept her television on and tuned to CNN. The picture of Jim kneeling in the desert in that orange jumpsuit with his shaved head and the black-masked executioner standing behind him filled the screen continuously that first day and night and day, and then the image was shrunk to a small square above Wolf Blitzer's head, which was somehow worse, and I wanted to scream at them all: "*He's not a news story!*" I'd have to jump up and go outside for a walk. Most often when I communicated with Shauna or Erin or Brian in those first days, I was walking on my parents' country road. I did that for hours, half a mile to the highway, half a mile back, over and over, in the sweltering khaki Oklahoma heat, the image of Jim kneeling in the desert repeating itself in my mind as relentlessly as the endless news loops, so that I was in a state of perpetual horror and grief. It was an early smoky dawn, I remember, the oaks and cedars emerging ghostlike from the mist with the orange-red sun rising as I walked in the cool dampness and felt for the first time a great sense of peace. I'd awakened that morning with the recognition that Jim was not caught for eternity in that terrible moment, only we were.

Erin and I spoke on the phone later that day, and I told her this, and she said, "Yes, yes, I've been thinking just that." I was standing at the crest of the hill on my parents' road, I remember, looking at High Peak Mountain east of Red Oak, saying, "He's not suffering anymore. He's at peace. He's not hurting." Erin and I kept saying it to each other, over and over, believing it. Trying to believe.

When it happened, James Foley's murder was the second most highly recognized event in U.S. history after 9/11, it is said. His death belongs to the world now, to history. His life belongs to his family and the friends who loved him. I began to have an idea of how many friends Jim had and the incredible number of lives he'd touched when I went to his memorial service near his home in New Hampshire, on a brilliant October day not unlike that bright September afternoon in Amherst when we all met. Jim's memorial was the first time since our last writing weekend in the Catskills that we'd all been together, Shauna and Erin and Brian and I, coming together in a lovely, large Catholic church, the faith Jim was raised in, along with so many hundreds of others, celebrating Jim's life on what would have been his forty-first birthday. The gathering afterward is when I learned for sure what I'd known in my heart but dreaded to know with certainty:

that Jim was indeed tortured. That, in fact, he was singled out for the worst tortures, the most terrible suffering, because he was American. What we as a country had done in Iraq and around the world had devolved onto Jim. And I learned, too, from those who had been held captive with him, how under the worst tortures and suffering and deprivation, Jim showed that moral courage he'd talked about at Marquette—and not just courage, but those other attributes Faulkner described in his Nobel speech: love and honor and pity and pride and compassion and sacrifice. And faith. Faulkner didn't speak of faith, but those who'd suffered with Jim did; they told us he never stopped believing that one day he would be freed. I don't think any of us, including Jim himself, ever dreamed in our worst imaginings that it would end the way it did.

In May 2015, seven months after the memorial, I had a dream about him. Next morning, I wrote this letter to Shauna and Brian and Erin:

> I dreamed about Jim last night. I was inside my house in the Catskills where you all visited that spring. I looked out the mud-room windows to the north and saw an older model sedan parked in the yard, Jimmy in the passenger seat, his brother, who looks so much like him, behind the wheel. My heart caught. I thought, That looks like Jim! But I knew it couldn't be. Still there was that feeling of warmth. I hurried around, putting on makeup, preparing for something, and then I went to a large public room on the south side of the cabin (you know dream language—an impossible place but perfectly logical in the dream), and it was a welcome home party for Jim. He'd just been released. I looked around for you three, for others I knew, but saw only strangers. But they were good, kind strangers, people who loved him and were so glad to have him returned, like the many from all his different walks of life at the memorial, people I didn't know but felt a connection to because they were connected to Jim, and loved him. You three weren't there, Diane and John weren't there, but his siblings were. And Jim standing in the middle of everything, smiling, his hair long and kind of shaggy, and he was so thin, wraithlike nearly, hollowed out from all he had suffered. Paul was wanting me to leave, he was

calling to me, so I went to Jim to tell him goodbye. I reached up to hug him, and he was tall, as he always was tall, but bone thin, his shoulders fragile beneath my hands, it was like hugging my frail 90-year-old dad, and yet there was, radiating from him, a powerful, benevolent love and a profound sorrow, not for his own suffering but for ours. He knew and sorrowed over the suffering others had suffered on his behalf. He knew, and was as powerless over what had happened to him as any of us were, and it grieved him beyond sorrow. I will never forget that radiant feel of grief and love. Yes, I know it's a Christ figure, I know it's a symbol from deep in my psyche, I know how dreams work. But I know, too, somehow, also, that it was Jim.

It seems like a profound narrative arc, meeting Jim Foley and those other young writers, working with them the first time on the night before 9/11, and the years in between like a bridge from that hugely public national devastation to the private devastations we each went through, and shared, thirteen years later when we learned about Jim's death. And yet that second devastation was so infamously public, too. Our piece of the national narrative. The piece I have to tell is only what I thought and feared during those years of silence when we didn't know what had happened to him, and the connection I felt with him and three other writers whose lives intersected mine the day before 9/11, and are connected there still. Erin and Brian and Shauna each have their piece, their memories, their special relationship to Jim. My small piece is glancing, caught just at the edge, akin to that day in August 2001 when I tried to go with my friend Connie to see Geronimo's grave, akin to hearing Marlene describe on the phone running for her life, hiding, choking in the black smoke from the crumbling World Trade Center—akin to how each of us bears witness to lived history, unfolding at close range or a great distance, whether we recognize it or not. We tell our stories, so many of us, as if they take place outside of time, outside of history. We think the world's stories are just there, on the outside, bordering our lives' true narrative, breaking in only from time to time if the magnitude and horror are great enough. But history, both present and past, is always impinging on our lives, whether we tell the truth of it, or deny it, or believe it.

On the plane back to Oklahoma after Jim's memorial, I met six young recruits on their way to basic training at Fort Sill. Our flight was delayed in Newark, so we sat on the tarmac quite a while—long enough for me to get the drift of their stories: they'd all signed up together, six young men from New Jersey, just out of high school, nervous and hopped up, simultaneously looking forward to and dreading what they'd find in the army, goofing with each other, kidding around. I smiled, listening to them—they struck me the same way the young writers in Amherst struck me in 2001: the best of what's best in us, so very completely American—though this was surely a more diverse bunch: two white boys, two Asian American boys, one Latino, one African American, who had a honeyed smile like my godson's and kept calling me ma'am. I told them I was from Oklahoma, I'd been to Lawton, I thought maybe they were going to like Fort Sill. "It's beautiful," I said. This did not impress them. They wanted to know about the weather "out there": was it really as fucking cold as people said? "Oh, excuse me, pardon me, ma'am, freaking cold, I mean."

"It's not bad," I said. "Not nearly as bad as upstate New York."

They weren't much impressed with that comment, either.

One of the two white boys sat across the aisle from me. He was really a handsome kid, tall and lean, with a thick shock of brown hair and the same kind of all-American good looks Jim Foley had. He'd never flown before, and he was obviously more than just nervous. He was, in fact, you could tell, quite scared. The other guys wouldn't let up on him, especially his white compatriot, seated in the next row forward but turned around to face us, leaning over the seat back while we waited on the tarmac, busting this kid's chops; he tried to bring me in on the kidding, explaining how his friend here had never been on a plane before, and he was scared shitless—oh, pardon me, ma'am—but you watch, dude, after this he's going airborne, he's going to be an effing paratrooper, you watch, and the others laughed. The kid tried to laugh with them, tried to laugh at them, told them to shut the fuck up, but none of it was working. They weren't letting up, and he was still scared.

He's going to be the one, I said to myself, watching him. He'll be the soldier wrapping a dog leash around the neck of a naked Iraqi prisoner. The intelligence officer shoving a cloth over a prisoner's mouth, pouring in the water. He's the one with the most imagination, and thus

the most fear. When he gets to the war zone, wherever that's going to be, he'll be the one who lashes out the most cruelly. The worst of what's best and worst in us—the most American in that way, too.

Our plane took off finally, and the boy pulled his jacket over his head and pretended to sleep the whole flight, but I don't believe he was sleeping. When we landed in Houston hours later, at George Bush Intercontinental Airport, we had to take the tram around to our separate gates for our connecting flights—they to Lawton–Fort Sill Regional Airport, I to Fort Smith. It was quite late by then, the airport nearly empty, our reflections eerie in the windows of the lighted tram. In my mind I could see where they were headed, the handsome, orderly base with its winding curves and tended lawns, its pale walls and red tile roofs. Its history. I said, "Hey, you guys, when you get to Fort Sill, you ought to go see Geronimo's grave."

"Who's that?" the nervous white kid said.

"Aw, man, don't you know?" his white buddy derided him. "He's an Indian. The dude's famous, man. Geronimo-o-o!"

"He was Apache," I said. "A prisoner of war at Fort Sill. You can visit the jail where they held him, and his grave is there. And, yeah, he was famous—the most famous Apache ever. Probably the most famous prisoner of war."

"Well, hell," the kid said. "No wonder I don't know about him. I don't care about that. I only care about American prisoners of war."

I think about those young men from time to time. They've long since finished their basic training, long since left Oklahoma. They're out there stationed in whatever places around the globe the U.S. military is doing, at this moment, what it does. I wonder what they thought of Fort Sill when they got there, or if they ever went to see Geronimo's grave. It still cuts me hard to think of that young white man blurting out that this most powerful of Native American warriors, Geronimo, was not American at all. I feel that I know what "American" means to that kid, because it's what it meant to me as a kid growing up here, seeing the world, as I did, through a prism of whiteness. I hope I was wrong about the other things I thought about him. Hope I was wrong in fancying he might act out the worst part of our nature. I wasn't wrong about his fear, I know that, but maybe I was wrong about what he will do because of it.

Trouble is, I come from this place where fear has made people do terrible things, made us enact laws of segregation and anti-immigration, made us riot and murder and commit other kinds of unspeakable violence—and not fear only, of course, but also greed and power and dominance and other not lesser sins. But I carry hope, too, for the very reason that I grew up in this place, where people do come forward in generosity and self-sacrifice and hard work—that Oklahoma standard people talk about. Not always, but sometimes, those worst sins are balanced here by the better part of human nature—the best of what's worst and best in us. Balanced, at least, and maybe even outweighed.